THE SOCRATIC WISDOM

THINK WITH CLARITY, SPEAK WITH PRECISION, AND ACT WITH INTEGRITY THROUGH THE TIMELESS LESSONS FROM THE LIFE OF SOCRATES

WISDOM UNIVERSITY

CONTENTS

For Our Readers — 1

What Readers Are Saying About Wisdom University — 9

Introduction — 13

1. The Wisdom Of A Beginner's Mind — 18
How Socrates Maintained A Childlike Wonder Throughout His Life And Why You Should Too

2. Do You Know That You Don't Know? — 30
The Pitfall Of Superiority Complex And Socrates' Antidote To Complacency

3. Your 5 Keys To Unlocking Socrates — 43
Rundown Of The Different Socratic Schools For A Well-Rounded Life

4. The Man Who Shunned Writing — 57
Why Socrates Preferred Speech Over Writing And How You Can Adopt The Secrets Of Socrates' Conversational Power

5. Enough Is Enough — 69
Discover The Perfect Balance Of Knowledge With Xenophon's Socratic Guide To A Flourishing Learning Journey

6. Plato's Socrates — 83
How To Know Yourself, What We Should Share With Our Friends, And Why We Can Find Peace If We Get To The Bottom Of Things

7. Have You Ever Been The Butt Of The Joke? — 95
Socrates According To Aristophanes And How To Identify The Line Between Slander And Constructive Criticism

8. The Trial Of Socrates — 108
An Example Of Unflinching Philosophy, Unyielding Resolve, And Unshakeable Integrity In A World Of Accusations

9. Socrates' Blueprint To Real Happiness   127
   How To Embrace Virtue, Build Holistic Character, Gain Inner Wealth, And Find Joy Beyond The Ephemeral
10. Who's The Wisest Of Them All?   141
    The Legacy Of The Gadfly Philosopher And His Gift Of Unflinching Questions For Both Ancient And Modern Critical Thinkers

Afterword   149
Over 10,000 People Have Already Subscribed. Did You Take Your Chance Yet?   155
The People Behind Wisdom University   157
References   163
Disclaimer   173

Get 100% Discount On All New Books!

Get ALL our upcoming eBooks for FREE
(Yes, you've read that right)
Total Value: $199.80*

You'll get exclusive access to our books before they hit the online shelves and enjoy them for free.

Additionally, you'll receive the following bonuses:

Bonus Nr. 1

Our Bestseller
How To Start Mind Mapping
Total Value: $9.99

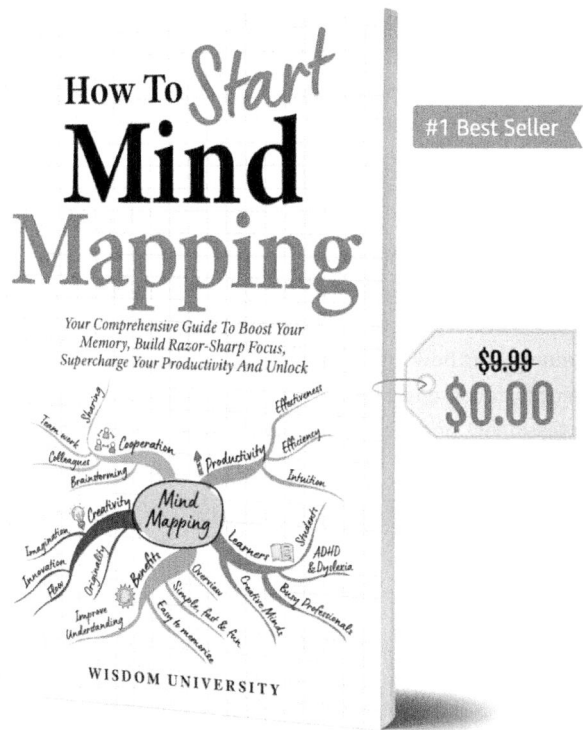

Do you ever feel like your brain is overloaded?

Like there's too much information swirling around and you can't keep track of it all?
Introducing mind mapping – a powerful tool that lets you visualize your thoughts!
This book is packed with step-by-step guides that show you exactly how to create mind-blowing mind maps for any subject or task.

"This book is an excellent resource for anyone interested in improving their cognitive skills and boosting productivity through mind mapping. It offers clear, step-by-step instructions on how to get started with mind mapping, making it accessible even for beginners. The guide is well-organized and covers everything from the basics to advanced techniques, helping readers unlock their full creative potential."

HK007 - Reviewed in the United States on August 12, 2024

"The book offers a thorough introduction to mind mapping. There are clear, step-by-step instructions that make the technique accessible to beginners and valuable for seasoned users. It demonstrates how mind mapping can significantly improve memory, focus, and productivity. Good read for students, professionals, and lifelong learners aiming to unlock their full potential."

Passionate - Reviewed in the United States on August 7, 2024

"This is a great book for people wanting to improve memory and cognitive abilities!"

Lisa - Reviewed in the United States on August 12, 2024

"This book is your ticket to turning chaos into creativity. Perfect for students, professionals, or anyone looking to upgrade their mental toolkit, 'How To Start Mind Mapping' will teach you how to map your way to brilliance. With scientific backing and real-world success stories, this isn't just another productivity hack – it's a mental game-changer. Cannot wait to put it to practice!"

@Msrexti - Reviewed in the United States on August 16, 2024

Bonus Nr. 2

Our Bestseller
The Art Of Game Theory
Total Value: $9.99

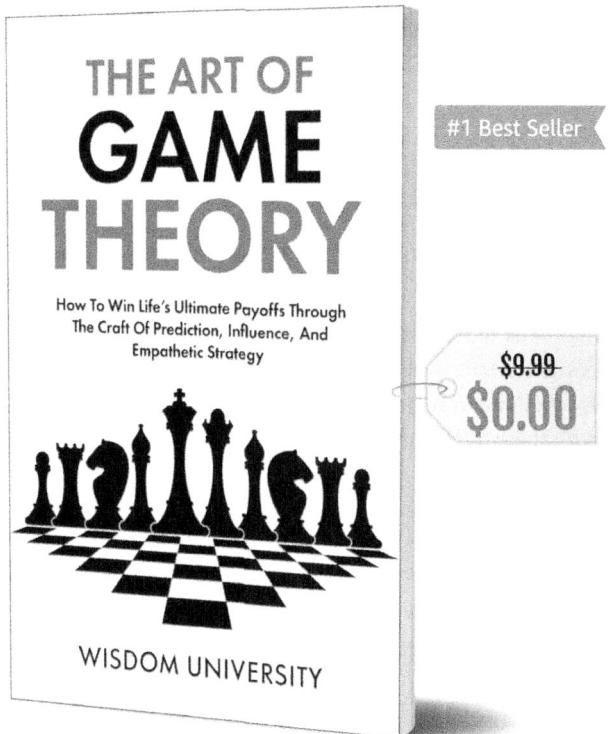

Step into the fascinating world of game theory with *The Art Of Game Theory*!

This expertly written book for beginners will introduce you to strategic decision-making and show you how game theory applies to diverse fields in clear and simple terms.

Whether you're a student, professional, or lifelong learner, *The Art Of Game Theory* equips you with powerful tools to gain a strategic edge in life.

"Thanks Wisdom University! This book offers simple strategies one can use to achieve things in your personal life. Anyone of average intelligence can read, understand and be in a position to enact the suggestions contained within."

David L. Jones - Reviewed in the United States on November 12, 2023

"Haven't finished it yet, but what I've gone through so far is just incredible! Another great job from this publisher!"

W. S. Jones - Reviewed in the United States on October 12, 2023

"A great book to help you through difficult and complex problems. It gets you to think differently about what you are dealing with. Highly recommend to both new and experienced problem solvers. You with think differently after reading this book."

Thom - Reviewed in the United States on October 18, 2023

"I like this book and how it simplifies complex ideas into something to use in everyday life. I am applying the concept and gaining a lot of clarity and insight."

Ola - Reviewed in the United States on October 18, 2023

"The book is an excellent introduction to game theory. The writing is clear, and the analysis is first-rate. Concrete, real-world examples of theory are presented, and both the ways in which game theory effectively models what actually happens in life is cogently evaluated. I also appreciate the attention paid to the ethical dimensions of applying game theory in many situations."

Amazon Customer - Reviewed in the United States on October 8, 2023

Bonus Nr. 3 & 4

Thinking Sheets
Break Your Thinking Patterns
&
Flex Your Wisdom Muscle
Total Value Each: $4.99

A glimpse into what you'll discover inside:
- How to expose the sneaky flaws in your thinking and what it takes to fix them (the included solutions are dead-simple)
- Dozens of foolproof strategies to make sound and regret-free decisions leading you to a life of certainty and fulfillment
- How to elevate your rationality to extraordinary levels (this will put you on a level with Bill Gates, Elon Musk and Warren Buffett)
- Hidden gems of wisdom to guide your thoughts and actions (gathered from the smartest minds of all time)

Here's everything you get:

- ✓ How To Start Mind Mapping eBook ($9.99 Value)
- ✓ The Art Of Game Theory eBook ($9.99 Value)
- ✓ Break Your Thinking Patterns Sheet ($4.99 Value)
- ✓ Flex Your Wisdom Muscle Sheet ($4.99 Value)
- ✓ All our upcoming eBooks ($199.80* Value)

Total Value: $229.76

Go to wisdom-university.net for the offer!

(Or simply scan the code with your camera)

*If you download 20 of our books for free, this would equal a value of 199.80$

WHAT READERS ARE SAYING ABOUT WISDOM UNIVERSITY

"I have been reading books from Wisdom University for a while now and have been impressed with the CONDENSED AND VALUABLE INFORMATION they contain. Reading these books allows me to LEARN INFORMATION QUICKLY AND EASILY, so I can put the knowledge to practice right away to improve myself and my life. I recommend it for busy people who don't have a LOT of time to read, but want to learn: Wisdom University gives you the opportunity to easily and quickly learn a lot of useful, practical information, which helps you have a better, more productive, successful, and happier life. It takes the information and wisdom of many books and distills and organizes the most useful and helpful information down into a smaller book, so you spend more time applying helpful information, rather than reading volumes of repetition and un-needed filler text.

—*Dawn Campo, Degree in Human psychology and Business, Office administrator from Utah*

"WU is a provider of books regarding mental models, thought processes, organizational systems, and other forms of mental optimization. The paradigmatic customer likely is to be someone in an early- to mid-career stage, looking to move up the ranks. Ultimately, though, the books could be of use to everyone from high school students to accomplished executives looking for ways to optimize and save time."

—Matthew Staples, 45, Texas (USA), Juris Doctor, Attorney

"I have most of the ebooks & audiobooks that Wisdom University has created. I prefer audiobooks as found on Audible. The people comprising Wisdom University do an excellent job of providing quality personal development materials. They offer value for everyone interested in self-improvement."

—*Neal Cheney, double major in Computer-Science & Mathematics, retired 25yrs USN (Nuclear Submarines) and retired Computer Programmer*

"I would recommend these books to my grandson."

—Daniel, Florida (USA), 69, Bachelor Degree, retired

"Wisdom University embodies an innovative and progressive educational approach, expertly merging deep academic insights with contemporary learning techniques. Their books are not only insightful and captivating but also stand out for their emphasis on practical application, making them a valuable resource for both academic learning and real-world personal development."

—*Bryan Kornele, 55 years old, Software Engineer from the United States*

"WU's emails discuss interesting topics. They have good offers. I can recommend the books to my My friends and relatives."

—Wilbur Dudley, Louisiana (USA), 77, BS in Business Administration and DBA, retired

"I wanted to read some books about thinking and learning which have some depth. I can say "Wisdom University" is one of the most valuable and genuine brands I have ever seen. Their books are top-notch at kindle. I have read their books on learning, thinking, etc. & they are excellent. I would especially recommend their latest book "Think Like Da Vinci" to those who want to have brilliant & clear thinking."

—*Sahil Zen, 20 years old from India, BSc student of Physics*

"Wisdom University's works provide a synthesis of different books giving a very good summary and resource of self-help topics. I have recommended them to someone who wanted to learn about a topic and in the least amount of time."

—Travvis Mahrer, BA in Philosphy, English Teacher in a foreign country

INTRODUCTION

If there is one overwhelming goal that all our desires and actions aim at, it is our personal happiness. If there is anything we have learned from experience, it is that life interrupts, delays, and complicates achieving this goal of happiness. Life is at once something that happens to us, but it is also something we do—we are active participants shaping our own lives.

The challenges we face in our lives are unique in one sense but also general to all mankind. In this book, we will look at Socrates' life, a life filled with wisdom that still applies today. What Socrates tells us about life can be seen in two important ways, what he did (his deeds) and what he said (his words). In the figure of Socrates, we see what we all admire—a man who was able to unite his convictions with his actions. What he aspired to, he lived, believing a life without regret is a life with purpose.

This book is meant to help you on the path toward achieving goals in your personal and professional life. Just as a journey cannot be made without thousands of steps, so a full life is composed of many distinct activities. Socrates came from a different time and place than our modern world. But the concerns he had, as well as the problems he faced, the aims he aspired to, and the actions he undertook, are features common to humans everywhere.

You may have read about Socrates in a Platonic dialogue in college. Now you can learn more about this captivating figure. It turns out this philosopher was not only interested in obscure aspects of speculation; above all, he took an interesting approach to living life and living life well. This is not unlike your own life, for if you were not interested in living well like Socrates, you would not pick up books like this to improve yourself.

Do not think that because Socrates lived in the classical age of Athens, he was living it up all the time at drinking parties. Socrates lived a hard life. He had a reputation for often walking around barefoot, which is a good indication of the general poverty he experienced. He was ridiculed and held in contempt by some of his fellow citizens he would engage in conversation with. He was put on trial for trumped-up charges. All things considered, Socrates lived a life of difficulties and challenges. He is someone with the wisdom of experience we can all learn from. Our critical thinking and our practical activities can both be helped immensely by Socrates' example.

There is a way in which Socrates cuts an entirely comforting figure because he, too, endured hardships and setbacks in life. But there is another factor at work, and this is the new perspective he offers. Socrates is from a foreign world and an unfamiliar time, with a mindset utterly different than any we are accustomed to. This fresh vantage allows Socrates to advise us across the ages, to remind us that we as humans have common experiences and can approach them in uncommon ways.

Some of our problems may have to do with money, some with stress, and others with time management. Socrates deals with all these in one way or another, but his overriding concern is with the person. Rather than complexity, the Socratic approach focuses on simplicity. This does not mean it is easy, but it means the conditions of success are plain and open. Seeking happiness above all, focusing on the important things, pursuing the cultivation of virtue, always thinking our actions through, and acknowledging our limitations are some of the principles we inherited from Socrates, and he had a unique perspective on understanding and putting them into effect. We begin by knowing ourselves, our ignorance and limitations, our motivations and desires, and we end with achieving excellence.

The holistic perspective that Socrates offers focuses on self-examination and the simplification of our concerns. The key to improving yourself, your outlook, and your life situation always begins with yourself. *You* have the agency to affect these changes, and with help from this book, you will have the knowledge to get there.

It should comfort—and encourage—you to know that the problems you face are not dissimilar from what all people, including Socrates, experience. One way to state this is that life is always in flux. Things are always changing; sometimes those changes are good, sometimes they're bad, yet often they are neutral. But we need stability as well. The ideas and methods in this book are designed to infuse that stable element we all need in life into your character. As we will see from Socrates, assurance and confidence in life are not lived in isolation from others. Friends, family, loved ones, and co-workers all work together for a life worth living.

You may be thinking to yourself, why should I read this book? Isn't it about a dead old guy who lived long ago? But you will be shocked at the insights that Socrates will give you. In my years of investigation as a PhD researcher at the University of Chicago, I have never encountered a human being in real life with as much wisdom as this old philosopher who lived more than two millennia ago. And I am sure you will come to agree.

This book is not about giving you the easiest solutions. After all, some of Socrates' greatest insights come from his trial and death. Instead, it will illuminate approaches and give you insights and techniques for dealing with life and its challenges. Socrates believed that all practical concerns, the parts of life that have to do with taking action, should begin with the mind. The mind rules the body, and so all decisions and actions should be guided by the mind. And just as the mind comes before the body, the child comes before the wise adult. If you are ready to start learning about Socrates and how his philosophy first took shape, then turn to Chapter 1.

1

THE WISDOM OF A BEGINNER'S MIND

HOW SOCRATES MAINTAINED A CHILDLIKE
WONDER THROUGHOUT HIS LIFE AND WHY YOU
SHOULD TOO

Do you think of a philosopher as someone who is exceedingly serious and maybe even pretentious? Maturity and wisdom, you might think, are the hallmarks of the philosopher, and therefore a philosopher cannot be childlike. But Socrates was always asking questions, always seeking out answers and knowledge from others. Plato says that philosophy begins in wonder,[1] and Socrates was always full of wonder.

This childlike wonder and curiosity can be seen throughout the accounts we have of Socrates in Plato, the philosopher; Xenophon, the historian; and Aristophanes, the comic playwright. In Plato's dialogues, written as interactions between different characters, the origin of many great philosophical investigations begins with a rather simple question by Socrates: What is "It" or What is X? The structure of entire dialogues comes from answering variations of that simple question: What is justice? *Republic*. What is courage? *Laches*. What is knowledge? *Theaetetus*. What is being? *Sophist*. The consequences of this very simple question have been profound for philosophy. Yet this is also the question of a child. And in fact, we will find out that the average person in Athens reacted to Socrates in a way very similar to how many people treat children who ask too many questions. His questions exasperated his fellow citizens because they found them so perplexing, and the sheer quantity—there was a doggedness in Socrates in pressing his fellow citizens for answers. Socrates was pesky in the eyes of the public and this earned him the reputation of a gadfly, a large biting insect that annoys livestock.

From one perspective it was this insatiable curiosity and quest for truth that both gave Socrates his purpose and led to his eventual execution. But what we will also see is that Socrates used the information and experiences available to him and turned them into knowledge. Now, Socrates' circumstances might be different from your own. He thought of himself as conducting philosophical conversations because of a divine mandate, which is unlikely to match what you think of doing in your own life. But the Socratic insight will be the same: You can take what you learn in one area of life and use it to understand things in a completely different area.

Socrates' early life

We do not possess a lot of information about Socrates in his youth. This is partly due to Plato's preference to write dialogues depicting an older Socrates. But we know that

Socrates' father was Sophroniscus, a stonemason, and that the odds are very good that Socrates was himself trained in this same craft.[2] Perhaps Socrates himself fashioned some of the stone facades which can still be seen in Athens today. There are frequent discussions in the Platonic dialogues of different arts, and we can be relatively certain that the views Socrates gives in the dialogues represent his thinking on art spurred in part by his experience with his stonemason father. In the later dialogue "Laws," Plato relates the stonemason's maxim that "big stones are not well laid without little stones."[3] Since Plato was from an aristocratic family, an unlikely source of such a maxim, it is reasonable that he learned this blue-collar wisdom from Socrates himself.

In "Phaedo," Plato tells us that a young Socrates was already reading the philosophy of Anaxagoras. Literacy was commonplace by the time of Socrates, although Ancient Greece had been preliterate for a time before then. Although he left no written words of his teachings, he was in no way illiterate or uneducated. In the same dialogue, in fact, we are told that Socrates was putting Aesop's Fables into poetic form as a kind of intellectual exercise.[4]

His mother, Phaenarete, was a midwife. In the dialogue "Theaetetus," Socrates tells us about her, and asks Theaetetus, "And have you also heard that I practise the same art?"[1] He goes on to tell us that he is like a midwife in that he helps others bear forth offspring. But what he brings forth are not children of the body, but children of the soul, that is, ideas and thoughts. Just as midwives are past childbearing age, so Socrates, as he claims, is past the age for having ideas—but he can help others bring forth their own offspring, testing the offspring, as does a midwife, to ensure their health. He can also determine, as a midwife of the soul, whether it is better to induce a miscarriage, if the idea would not be beneficial. This strange and striking metaphor of the midwife is also different in an ultimate way, Socrates tells us, because it is performed on men and not women.

Socrates saw in midwifery a number of skills and practices that he could apply to philosophy: helping others although unable to bear offspring himself, promoting the welfare of those he engaged with, producing intellectual "offspring," and fostering the right outcome for these intellectual offspring.

From his upbringing, we can see that his parents' occupations played an influential role in the way Socrates viewed the world and his role in it. Although he was engaged in a different task, he was still able to bring his early experience to help guide and understand what he was doing as an older man. We can see this more clearly in his mother's case, as Socrates chose to pursue his philosophical activities with the seriousness, compassion, and best welfare of his "patients" in mind.

What we see in Socrates' early life is that he was using whatever framework he had available to him at the time as a stepping stone to learn even more. Socrates tapped into a profound yet simple truism: Even when you have little knowledge you can develop what little knowledge you have into more. Knowledge is like a seed. It is something you must plant, water, and tend to. You cannot just stick seeds into your pocket and expect to grow an apple orchard. But what is relatively modest can be turned into something profound. Socrates was able to interpret the world around him through the simple analogy of his mother's midwifery. He applied what he saw to his own chosen task in life. Socrates' example challenges us: How can you use your past experience to guide your future insight?

If we look at other parts of his youth, Socrates always looked for exposure to new ideas, whether through interacting with people or just reading papyrus scrolls.

Socrates' experience was not limited to purely intellectual matters alone, but his life even from an early age was concerned with action. Athens of the Classical Age not only desired her young men to be strong in mind but strong in body, both intelligent and courageous. Just like all the other men of the time, Socrates would have had to serve for two years in the Athenian military.[5] During his service, Socrates engaged in several battles. Near Spartolus, Socrates saved Alcibiades from certain death,[6] and at Delium he was courageous in defeat, earning the praise of the general Laches in the dialogue of the same name.[7] Socrates was able to turn the lessons he learned about courage on the battlefield into the relatively peaceful field of philosophical inquiry. Socrates says that it takes the most courage to speak up in conversation.

Whether you agree with Socrates or not, there are several important parallels between military courage and social courage. There is the fear of public speaking, which many of us are familiar with, but there is also a certain level of confrontation involved when we speak to people. For example, we hold people accountable for promises, question whether their ideas are sound, and tell them when what they are saying is untrue—or at least we do when we are being courageous.

So just as we have seen with the midwife example, Socrates was using his experience from one area of life to help frame his understanding of another. Midwifery is not just for children and courage is not just for soldiers. Socrates applied his knowledge by transferring it creatively into new domains, and we can, too. This application of midwifery to philosophy not only helps to situate the new knowledge we are gaining, but importantly, it cements and clarifies the knowledge we already have.

For example, say you know what it takes to keep and maintain an aquarium. This knowledge about an aquarium can make it easier to understand what it takes to keep and maintain a terrarium or pets in general: the temperature parameters, cleaning, monitoring healthy behavior, feeding schedules, and the like. But it will not be until you transfer this knowledge to the case of the terrarium that you will really understand why you are doing what you are doing. You are not performing these actions for no reason; they have a real purpose to them—

to create a healthy and entertaining enclosure for animals. This feature common to both the aquarium and terrarium is real knowledge. It is durable, transferable, and applicable to a wide range of domains.

Knowledge transfer is a great foothold for gaining competency in other areas. A 2020 review of scientific literature channeling the application of university studies to the workforce found that knowledge occurs through channels, "media through which encoded knowledge is transferred (unidirectional)," and processes, "social configurations in which coded and encoded language is shared (multi-directional) with an increasing level of relational involvement."[8] Traditional channels include teaching and research, while processes include the transfers themselves through thought relationships and social application. Knowledge transfer can also occur between people—and even organizations. Interestingly, according to a 2022 analysis of 53 articles, social networks can provide ample opportunity for knowledge transfer. One social network survey covered in the analysis discovered that "workers embedded in a diverse knowledge clique" are better candidates for knowledge transfer because of the resources surrounding them, including other knowledgeable workers.[9] Apart from the "worker" qualifier, this perfectly describes Socrates and his associates.

Even within his chosen pursuit of philosophical discourse, Socrates was not always in control of the conversation. We also know that the young Socrates met up with the master philosopher Parmenides when he was just 19 years old. In the dialogue "Parmenides," Socrates puts up a valiant fight but he is taken to task by the wiser and more experienced Parmenides. In a turning of the tables, Parmenides asks young Socrates a number of questions he cannot quite answer.

How this one activity guided Socrates in everything

From this very general knowledge of Socrates' upbringing, we can already see a number of helpful lessons. One is the extremely important role of inquisitiveness, a trait often associated with children. We often are afraid of asking questions in today's society because it can suggest uncertainty or lack of comprehension in the questioner. But what we find in Socrates is that questions are the very source of knowledge. Without questions, we do not expand or evaluate our experiences or develop new areas to explore in our lives.

One immediate application of question-asking is in the realm of curiosity. We can define curiosity in different ways, but at its heart, it involves what is of interest to us. We are curious about things that capture our attention—we think about them. And curiosity, Socrates shows us, is not something that just strikes us out of the blue like a lightning bolt. It can be cultivated, increased, and even rewarded, by asking questions. Socrates would not even care if there was such a thing as a dumb question because, even if there were, he would be on to the next question, and the next, and the one after that. Asking questions always generates more questions. So what happens is that as you ask more questions, you become more curious.

Questions are a creative process because you can take them wherever you want. Remember, Socrates always began simply, for example, with, "What is justice?" in the "Republic." But then he transformed this simple question into a complex city-state with three different classes corresponding to three parts of the soul. Questions lead to more questions, but they also lead to more creativity, more complexity, and more interest in what you are learning about. Some people think that questioning challenges authority and societal order and that raising questions is a way of raising doubt about what is being questioned. This is certainly what some of Socrates' contemporaries thought. But the heart of Socratic questioning is not deconstructive but constructive. Questions grant new insights and allow for creativity.

Socrates found many opportunities to apply the insights he found within his philosophy—and even transfer knowledge. In Xenophon's work "Memorabilia," which relates interesting sayings and activities of Socrates, we see him advising the two quarreling brothers Chaerophon and Chaerecrates. Gently he advises Chaerecrates, "If you try to manage a horse without knowing the right way, he hurts you. Is it so with a brother? Does he hurt if you try to deal with him when you don't know the way?"[10] Chaerecrates doesn't answer the question, instead petulantly turning the discussion back to his brother's misbehavior as a child likely would. But Socrates won't let him digress: "Had you a sheep dog that was friendly to the shepherds, but growled when you came near him, it would never occur to you to get angry, but you would try to tame him by kindness. You say that, if your brother treated you like a brother, he would be a great blessing, and you confess that you know how to speak and act kindly: yet you don't set yourself to contriving that he should be the greatest possible blessing to you."[10] Here, Socrates applies his knowledge of good treatment of animals to people, his imagination combining different areas of his life to make sense of them. In this anecdote from Xenophon about Socrates, we see that knowledge transfer was the key to understanding how to deal with quarreling brothers.

Action steps

What are some of the areas in which you already have knowledge? This can be from hobbies or jobs, or any experience which has given you insight into the world. Now, what are some areas you want to learn about? Are there similarities in the two areas so that your experience can help you learn? Are tools required in your previous area of knowledge, like an auto mechanic or an artist? If so, what kind of tools are there in the area of knowledge you wish to learn about? Is there some product that comes out of your knowledge (e.g., in the case of a midwife, a child)? What you know about this process of production might apply to new areas of interest.

Whatever your area of knowledge, do not just let it sit there unconnected to the rest of your life. Start asking questions unselfconsciously. Do you know how to ride a bike but not how to operate a sewing machine? Ask yourself or others about similarities in parts (such as the foot pedal) and do a little research to determine if this similarity in function leads to any similarities in how you work the respective machines. You can perform this step for just about anything that shares similar parts: an oven and a pottery kiln, or a computer and a Jacquard loom. What can you determine based on what you know about both of them, gleaned through questions and independent research?

Socrates brought a youthful enthusiasm and curiosity to his whole life. He was always asking what something was, interacting with others, and growing in knowledge just like children do. To open ourselves to the world like Socrates we need to open up our childlike wonder as we approach the world. Next, we will see that prompted by the oracle at Delphi, Socrates had an insatiable desire to talk to everyone, to see what wisdom each person could share.

Chapter summary

- Socrates believed that knowledge began from

questions, ended with more questions, and was filled with creativity and insight throughout.
- Learning proceeds from the simple to the complex and from the familiar to the unfamiliar.
- Socrates was able to take simple information from one area of life and transfer it to new areas, like using his mother's profession of midwifery to guide his own understanding of the world or using his war experience to understand philosophy—a habit we can echo to reach a stepping stone to new areas.
- Interest and curiosity arise from asking questions; if you wait for something to become interesting to you, it may never occur because you first have to uncover the questions that lead to your interest.
- Socrates maintained a childlike wonder throughout his life, promoting creative questioning, which we all have as children but lose due to disuse and social discouragement.

2

DO YOU KNOW THAT YOU DON'T KNOW?

THE PITFALL OF SUPERIORITY COMPLEX AND SOCRATES' ANTIDOTE TO COMPLACENCY

How ignorance creates knowledge

Have you ever Googled a word or a question and received the answer "I don't know"? We live in an age in which we have become accustomed to immediate answers at our fingertips. We not only have *an* answer but, usually, Google responds with thousands or tens of thousands of answers. But for Socrates, the first step to knowledge is not an abundance of answers but a complete lack of them. Ignorance is the first step to knowledge. This sounds outrageous and almost offensive. But it's true. If you want to learn something, you first have to admit you lack the knowledge you seek. But in order to admit your ignorance, you have to know *about* your ignorance.

This chapter is about this very thing, knowing what you know (or don't). Socrates famously confessed that he only knew that he knew nothing, an idea which we will explore in depth. Despite its apparent position as an obstacle to knowledge, knowing about your ignorance is like knowing your own limitations and abilities.

It is in Plato's "Apology" that Socrates relates the story of a friend of his, Chaerophon, traveling to the sacred oracle at Delphi to ask a question about Socrates. The oracle at Delphi was a priestess of the god Apollo who would enter a trance, offering up cryptic responses to questions. Chaerophon, as an admirer of Socrates, wanted to know if anyone was wiser than Socrates. The oracle, whose pronouncements were considered divine and infallible, answered that no one was wiser than Socrates.[1]

Socrates then went around Athens in an attempt to show that the oracle must be wrong since he did not consider himself wise at all. He went to the politicians first. As he himself put it, through Plato, "Neither of us really knows anything fine and good, but [the politician] thinks he knows something when he does not, whereas I, as I do not know anything, do not think I do either."[1] He went to the poets and tragedians and found that "there was hardly a man present [...] who would not speak better than they about the poems they themselves had composed"[1] due to being directly inspired by the gods and contributing scant artistic innovation themselves.

Next, Socrates visited the craftsmen of different trades. But like the poets, "because of practicing [their] art well, each one thought he was very wise in the other most important matters, and this folly of theirs obscured that wisdom."[1] Socrates concluded that he could find no one wiser than himself, but it was not because he was so wise, but rather because all the other Athenians were so unwise.

Why were they unwise? Socrates said that, in effect, he knew that he did not know anything, whereas the others professed to know a lot. When refuting the wisdom of the politician, Socrates noted that at least he didn't lay claim to things he couldn't possibly know. The poets and craftsmen were similarly lacking in wisdom.

So the first step to Socratic wisdom is to admit to yourself how much you do not know. This relates to the certainty we have, as well as the content of knowledge itself. It is a common mistake to be overconfident in what one knows, and this overconfidence can lead to stubbornly clinging to incorrect information or thinking you possess more information than you really do. There is even a contemporary term for this, the Dunning-Kruger Effect: "a metacognitive phenomenon of illusory superiority," according to a 2020 study.[2] The idea is that those with the least knowledge tend to overestimate their capabilities while even those with the most insight also tend to assess their knowledge incorrectly—by underestimating it. At any rate, the Dunning-Kruger Effect shows that there is generally a mismatch between what we know and what we *think* we know. This is because we only know one side of the story—the part concerned with knowledge—but we do not know the extent of our ignorance. One might say we are not aware of our ignorance because we cannot know what we do not know. If we did, it would be something we know, and not something we don't know!

Getting to know our ignorance

But a big problem arises from what we have discovered. How can we come to know, and correct, our ignorance, if it's something we cannot know? Socrates' example shows the way. Remember that in order to understand the limitations of his own wisdom, Socrates immediately set out to test the oracle by talking with others. The way to determine how capable you really are in a given field of knowledge is to talk with others in that same field.

Talking to others gives you insight into your knowledge in ways you simply cannot achieve on your own. You will be able to compare what you know to what they know. This comparison will enable you to assess your knowledge in a much more accurate fashion. If, in fact, they know more than you or vice versa, this will come across as you speak about the topic. But you cannot speak to just one person, as this is unlikely to give you an accurate picture of your abilities. Speaking to only one person might just make you arrogant if they know a lot less than you or lack confidence if they know a lot more.

Socrates' approach was to talk to as many people as he could, all from many different walks of life. This was to get as wide a perspective on an issue as he could, but it was also in order that he could probe into many different issues. Remember: You don't know what you don't know.

There might be knowledge of a kind you simply cannot imagine which would be of immense help to you. It could be business knowledge, personal knowledge, or general wisdom. The point is that you would never know about any of this left to yourself. You must go out and make contact with people and find out what they know.

Another important takeaway from Socrates and the oracle is that there is simply an immense amount of knowledge out there in the world. In more recent years this is chalked up to the illusion of explanatory depth, which posits that we often think we know more than we do about something until we try to explain it.[3] The way this is presented in Plato's "Apology" is that, relatively speaking, Socrates seemed to know nothing compared to what can be known about the world. This awareness of the limitations of his own knowledge, and that of his fellow Athenians, could not be brought out until he talked to them.

Socrates' report was somewhat dire, since he came to the conclusion that no one really has knowledge and to possess the highest form of knowledge is to admit one has no knowledge. But we do not need to accept Socrates' radical understanding of universal and total ignorance to apply his principle. What Socrates did is incredibly insightful. We can look at the practical way in which he worked out his principle. An acknowledgment of his own lack of knowledge forced him to look elsewhere, wherever it was, to acquire that knowledge. By constantly being reminded in his interactions with others that he did not possess an adequate grasp of what he sought, Socrates was always on the prowl for more information. The moment you think that you have all the answers, you have no incentive to discover more. On the other hand, to admit you are ignorant, or at least lacking in knowledge, is a motivational blessing. With this mindset, you are open to new ideas, opportunities, and possibilities.

This Socratic approach to knowledge is odd to us because it seems to involve a lack of self-assurance, as if one were to go around constantly doubting whether one was thinking the right thing. An article in *Harvard Business Review* suggests developing a more confident alter ego to overcome self-doubt,[4] and who better than Socrates himself, secure in his ability to keep asking questions?

A pair of 2010 studies in the *Journal of Experimental Social Psychology* unearthed an interesting phenomenon: Participants were rethinking their doubt in the face of doubt activation attempts, summarized by the statement "I'm not confident that I am insecure; therefore, I might be certain." This was Study 1, in which researchers manipulated Ohio State University students to produce confidence or doubt through an uncertainty prime (a list of words to be arranged into sentences or crossed out if they didn't fit). They assessed self-doubt with the causal uncertainty (CU) scale. Study 2 added a writing task and physical cues—head shaking or nodding—to doubt-primed groups, and the group receiving the doubt cue actually showed less doubt than the latter receiving the certainty cue.[5] Just as Socrates doubted the Oracle and had to verify its claims, we can use our doubt to develop more knowledge and reinforce what we do know.

What the Socratic approach really reveals is that our knowledge will always pale in comparison to the total knowledge available to us. The more we know, the greater the temptation to think it sufficient or, worse, that we know it all. Imagine a computer programmer who thinks she has more or less mastered everything she needs for her job. But then two or three years go by and she has failed to keep up with the changing technology of the profession. New programs and codes have come out, and she does not possess the ability to use them. The Socratic approach to knowledge would have helped her. To be humble in our possession of knowledge is to be open to knowledge while to be proud of our knowledge is to become closed off to new information.

When we realize that we know very little compared to what we can learn, the right response is not to sit on our hands because we are pitifully ignorant. Rather the idea is that an awareness of our ignorance is the spur to finding out. Consider yourself at work. You find yourself getting into the same problem over and over again. It may be related to technology, language, or corporate policy. It doesn't matter for our purposes. You can handle the situation in one of two ways. Either you can allow your ignorance to keep you in a state of helplessness and inaction, or you can use your ignorance to find out the cause of why you keep running into the same problem. Why does this happen? What kind of problem is it? To answer these questions you have to learn by asking questions. Remember, this isn't a one-person show. You have to go to others in your organization and talk with individuals. Just as Socrates talked to people from different walks of life, you have to approach different people at your work to gather the broadest possible understanding of the problem—and how to solve it.

In Socrates' day, he was limited to face-to-face, or in the case of the oracle, divine knowledge. Today we have other resources for human knowledge, including online newspapers, journals, and encyclopedias. Works that themselves list sources are the gold standard here. To cast the broadest net, you can also comb online forums, YouTube, and social media. You can and should tap into these more democratic, less scholarly sources, but always take care to verify what you read on sites where anything can be posted. Ideally, you do this with other reputable sources echoing the information.

You should not limit yourself except to practice reasonable restraint against mistruths, but be sure not to deem a claim unreliable simply because you disagree! The gaping potential for knowledge acquisition in ignorance makes for an exciting state; the many paths a person can take to closing knowledge gaps form an ideological frontier. In admitting you know that you do not know, you have no way of scoping out the knowledge you seek or who is going to possess it. In the context of your job, it is possible the person with the knowledge could be your boss or a co-worker who is less experienced than you.

Earlier it was said that humility is part of the process of knowledge. This is not only because one has to admit ignorance in order to become knowledgeable. It is also because we have to admit we can only find knowledge in and through other people. It can be a blow to the ego to concede that others know something that we do not. But the Socratic approach also provides good guidance on this as well. Socrates would talk to many people, not just one or two. When we seek the advice of many, it becomes apparent that we are not dependent on just one or two people. The Socratic approach takes information from many different sources, then extracts, simplifies, and combines it into knowledge. To get there, you must first admit that you do not possess all the answers, but that together with others you can come to an adequate grasp of the whole.

There is a flip side to the Socratic approach. The admission that we do not have all the answers, and compared to what we could know, we know very little, might be taken as a very pessimistic way of looking at the world. But this is not the lesson Socrates took from his own ignorance. What it did was prompt him to have an insatiable desire for more and more knowledge. Knowing you do not know is the antidote to complacency. As soon as you know that you do not know, you adopt the viewpoint that you can never rest on your laurels and never become satisfied with what you know or what you have accomplished. Knowing your own limitations, that you have but one human life restricted to living in one city and one age at a time, you will come to have considerable respect for tapping into the resources of all the other persons you have in your life.

Action steps

The first step to knowledge is the kind of self-examination that results in acknowledging your own limitations. As soon as you do this, you have created the motivation for knowledge. When you are certain you do not possess knowledge then the only remedy is to seek it out. But this requires being honest with yourself and also requires a way to assess your knowledge.

It can be difficult to gauge our own state of knowledge. Our ignorance is something, as we found out, we do not know. But this situation is not hopeless. We can measure ourselves by talking to those who do know something about the subject. By doing this, we can come to know just how much we really do know and adjust our efforts accordingly. And just as Socrates made efforts to talk to a wide variety of people to get as broad a perspective as possible, so must you.

Remember Googling an answer, which we began with? The problem with Googling an answer is that very often it gives us the appearance that our knowledge is limitless, that we have all the answers. But this is simply not true. Google is simply a repository of information, just like a book, or in Socrates' day, a papyrus scroll. By themselves, they possess no power to bring knowledge to you. In order to be effective sources of knowledge, you have to pick them up and read them.

Knowledge is not something so easy that it comes running to you at the click of a mouse or tap of a phone. You have to go after it, and this active process takes energy, effort, and focus. The acquisition of knowledge always begins with you, but it never really ends. You move on to the next problem, the next solution, and the next set of questions.

Think of at least one thing you know you don't know. Next comes a more challenging follow-up: Consider something you *think* you know. Are you superstitious over anything? Endorsing beliefs over facts for the moment will make this task easier, even if that's not something you want to do in general. You should not be able to find a definite endorsement or refutation of the latter claim; if you do, keep listing claims until you find one that isn't easily verified. Once you do, mentally cross it off the list of things you know, and rest assured that all that you need to do to add *true* knowledge back is ask more people more questions. Even if you can't arrive at a conclusive answer, chances are that you will attain partial knowledge by drawing on the wisdom of others.

In fact, a 2012 study used a "spanning tree memory task" to prompt short-term recall, analyzing individual solutions and the same solutions as an aggregate.[6] Researchers showed participants 25-node spanning trees, complex graphical images that they would later have to try to recreate on a computer themselves. The group solution outperformed individual ones because the aggregation method allowed for multiple people to (accurately) remember different parts of the spanning tree, providing a more complete picture and thus outperforming the average individual completing the memory task. The popularly-cited wisdom of crowds even held in complicated problems "requir[ing] the coordination of multiple pieces of information," proving yet more applicable than previously thought.[6]

Chapter summary

- Admitting your ignorance is the first step in the Socratic approach to knowledge, as Socrates did after learning from the oracle at Delphi that he was the wisest man alive because he was alone in knowing that he knew nothing.
- The Dunning-Kruger effect drives home the idea that we seldom have a good handle on our knowledge or abilities, making us susceptible to misinformation or disinformation. In order to raise ourselves above this vulnerability, we must look to others with whom we can compare our knowledge.
- We seek knowledge with as many people as we can for the sake of the quality of the knowledge itself, because the more perspectives we take into

consideration, the broader the view we will have of the whole.
- In one way, Socrates' insistence on not knowing anything can be understood as a way of expressing our relative ignorance. Even if we know a little more than nothing in actuality, we have such a limited perspective compared to what we *can* know that we should be all the more eager to take every opportunity to learn more from a greater variety of sources.
- The temptation we face in not acknowledging our own inadequate grasp of knowledge is complacency, or thinking we have every answer, which pushes us to neglect the questions.
- By facing our own limitations and admitting that we only have a small share in knowledge, we quickly look somewhere beyond ourselves as we seek the knowledge of others.

3

YOUR 5 KEYS TO UNLOCKING SOCRATES

RUNDOWN OF THE DIFFERENT SOCRATIC SCHOOLS FOR A WELL-ROUNDED LIFE

Socrates' branches of glory

In football, coaches' achievements are often interconnected by mentorship, not unlike that which is found in familial relationships. "Godfather of the NFL" Paul Brown earned a lasting legacy coaching future greats Lou Saban, Mac Speedie, and Bill Walsh.[1] In turn, Bill Walsh boasts mentees Sam Wyche, Dennis Green, and Ray Rhodes.[2] All this is charted in their coaching trees.

Though coaches are most associated with wins and losses, coaching trees are an even more significant measurement of success. The idea is that if a coach is really good, he is able to teach players to play well, but more importantly he can teach others how to coach. When a coach has multiple coaches who descend from his coaching tree, this is considered a sign of high success because the coach has proved to be more than just lucky, either with the players he has happened to have or with one or two bright students who turned out excellent coaches. If you have turned out multiple students who are noteworthy in their own right and innovative with their personal style, then you are really a significant figure.

When it comes to Socrates, despite his claims that he knew nothing and that was not a teacher, he left quite the mark as a "philosophical coach." Socrates' students—especially Plato and Aristotle—were notable in their own right, developing significant philosophical ideas through Socrates' inspiration.

As we have seen in previous chapters Socrates was an inquisitive philosopher. He was never satisfied with answers but always sought new knowledge and different questions. Considering his insistence that he was not a teacher, at least not intentionally, what happened with his students is somewhat expected.

Socrates' students founded different Socratic schools. Observing the various aspects of Socrates' philosophical personality, his students adopted and developed distinct lessons from the master. We will see that after the death of Socrates, his students took away different messages, depending on what they found to be the most important of his principles. Each of these principles represents an aspect of Socrates, and all together they form a fuller picture of Socratic life. By looking at them, we not only can come to understand Socrates better but also his approach to life. This is similar to talking to the children of a great person. Even if we never meet the person, his children are able to paint a portrait of him while giving us a glimpse of his wisdom.

We will focus on five Socratic schools, each imparting a different lesson for us to understand: Cynics, Megarians, Cyrenaics, Academic Skeptics, and Stoics.

The Cynics and valuing the internal

The Cynics were founded by one of Socrates' immediate disciples, Antisthenes. This Antisthenes was previously a disciple of Gorgias the sophist until he came into Socrates' orbit. In contrast to the ostentation of Gorgias, Socrates lived a humble and simple life. It was this factor that had the most impact on Antisthenes. Antisthenes sharply contrasted the idea of convention and nature. Convention is what people decide to arbitrarily do, while nature is what does not change.[3]

Antisthenes focused on what really mattered, and not the externals. In one anecdote from Laertius, Antisthenes is recorded as saying that the virtue of a statue is its beauty. But statues are inanimate, so it would be shameful for living humans to take their virtue from the same thing as statues.[4] The idea is that beauty is not as important as the virtues of the mind, and that we should focus on ornamenting our souls rather than our bodies.

This same principle applies to the words we use. Just as beauty is to the body so are words to deeds. The words we use are external, but they are not to be confused with the substance of actions. Real virtue is not to be found in the appearance of things but in the reality of them.

The lesson the Cynics give to us has a wide application. Whatever is only on the surface has little value, and we should be concerned with the heart and core of things. So actions matter more than words, virtue is greater than the conventional laws we see around us, the state of our mind is more valuable than the clothes we wear, and how we treat other people is of more importance than the customary social manners we have been taught.

Antisthenes and the students who followed him often indulged in dramatic efforts to demonstrate this principle. For example, Diogenes would walk around naked to flout convention.[5] But we need not concentrate on the more eccentric instances to take home the idea that what matters is not the external but the internal.

The Megarians and precision through conversation

Another Socratic school, the Megarians, was founded by Eucleides of Megara. We don't know much about them, mostly because their writings have been lost, but they held a reputation in antiquity for rigorous and logical thought. In contrast to the Cynics, who emphasized action, the Megarians were much more concerned with thought. Among other things, this resulted in a focus on precision in speech. In focusing on speech, they developed two further aspects of language: logic and the art of discussion or dialectic.[6] Logic is nothing more than clarifying what is meant, and determining whether it is true or false. This goes hand in hand with the art of dialectic, the process of going back and forth with someone in conversation. This emphasis on discussion shows the strong influence of Socrates whose question-and-answer format shaped the Megarians' own technique. The texts that arose out of this school were in dialogue form, with characters going back and forth, much like a Platonic dialogue.

The Megarians can teach us about the value of discussion when it comes to gaining knowledge, accomplishing a task, clarifying a concept, or even just having fruitful, meaningful conversations. The question-and-answer format has a number of practical benefits which can apply to any situation. There is the implicit assumption that there is a purpose to the conversation. We are discussing this because we imagine there to be an outcome: the resolution of a disagreement, clarification of a problem, or discovery of a more efficient method of accomplishing a task. Ancient Greece's tradition of dialectic can help bring balance and perspective when practiced today. Taking a breath and talking things through is a refreshing approach in an increasingly polarized world where ugly politicking ends friendships and even poses dangers when people get too fanatical.

In fact, a 2020 survey of twelve countries currently experiencing radicalized politics identified worsening trends in affective polarization, or distaste of political parties opposing yours, with the U.S. leaping up 5.6 percentage points every ten years since 1978 and topping out at over 50 percent.[7] In such divisive times, talking may be the only path to shared understanding. Still, for your own safety, try not to single out any hotheads for discussion. Unfortunately, some—like Thrasymachus in the "Republic"—are just quarrelsome and don't really want to discuss anything.

In addition to having purpose, question-and-answer discussions are also more precise because they are guided by a goal. Many conversations beat around the bush or traffic in insignificant banter. But a series of questions can be direct without being forceful. Compare the statement, "I think you did not finish your part of the project," with the question, "Did you finish your part of the project?" The question is not an accusation and is more open-ended, giving the person a chance to explain themselves.

The Megarians show us the value of question and answer in our dealings with others, and in turn, this leads to more precision in the context of working toward a respectful outcome.

The Cyrenaic focus on finding pleasure

The Cyrenaics are perhaps the most controversial of all of the Socratic schools because they focused on pleasure above all. Aristippus, their founder, taught that the purpose of life was pleasure, and not just any kind of pleasure, but the pleasure of the body in particular. Thus Aristippus is by any measure an extreme proponent of hedonism.[8]

The common accusation that hedonists are overindulgent and pampered does not seem to fit with what we know about Aristippus. Aristippus, Laertius tells us, "was capable of adapting himself to place, time and person, and of playing his part appropriately under whatever circumstances."[4] He also never went out of his way to seek pleasure, and this included future pleasures. Aristippus used whatever he had at hand to enter into a state of pleasure. This is very similar to the common adages that we should "make the best of what we have," or "bloom where you are planted."

The key to understanding how Aristippus can apply to us is not by focusing directly on his preoccupation with pleasure, but on the relationship between circumstances and what we can do. In Aristippus' view, we should not be constantly turning here and there in search of glutting ourselves with exotic new experiences, but instead, we should acknowledge that whatever situation we are in, there are pleasures to be had. When we do so, we come to realize that being content with what we have is not the same as forgoing any and all pleasure. Wherever we go there is something to take pleasure in. This is especially the case in the modern context, where there is always something to take pleasure in, even if it's something relatively familiar, like air conditioning, shelter, available and various food, or safety from violence.

We take all of these and more for granted every day and seldom have gratitude for these kinds of things. Taking pleasure in what we have also has other benefits: it keeps us frugal to maximize our resources, it spurs us to creatively make use of what we have, and calls us to assess our surroundings in terms of what has value to us and give our attention to it.

Academic skepticism and an open mind

The Academic Skeptics descend from the most famous pupil of Socrates, Plato. The first of these was Arcesilaus, who lived several generations after the death of Plato, and served as the head of the Platonic Academy for the last 25 years of his life.[9] Arcesilaus was especially interested in the Platonic dialogues where no certain conclusion is reached, the so-called "aporetic" dialogues. The emphasis for Arcesilaus was the suspension of judgment (*epochē*), or abandoning the assumption that you already know so you can observe experiences with new eyes.[10] He also prioritized the investigation of all sides of a topic. This thoroughness on a given issue meant that Arcesilaus had a profound depth of available information because he knew the benefits and drawbacks not only of one position but as many positions as there were on a given topic.

One way we can describe Arcesilaus' method is that his suspension of judgment allowed him to maximize his knowledge. That is, he first surveyed all the possible opinions and positions, and only afterward did he decide on them.

On mornings when you wake up on the wrong side of the bed before going to work, for example, it may be easier to pull your collar over your ears and push back against anyone who disagrees with you when you speak up at the weekly meeting. But if you suspend your judgment, you might find better ideas to replace or enhance your own. This will be impossible to see or fully appreciate if you have already made up your mind.

The Stoics and Socrates their guiding sage

The Stoic school looked up to Socrates as a sage and a man who had mastered the virtues of mind and ethics. So they valued the teachings of Socrates in which he explored the various Greek virtues. For the Stoic the goal of life was to live a life of virtue in accordance with nature.[11]

The Stoic ideal was so focused on virtue that they arrived at the radical belief that virtue was the only thing that mattered. The great Stoic lesson can be stated in very practical terms: There are things in our control and things out of our control. We can only focus attention on the things in our control, which is nothing other than virtue, so we simply do not need to worry about the things out of our control because they are out of our control.

In our daily lives, we might not have in mind the precise virtues of say, courage and justice, that the Stoics did. But even if not, we do have principles and values we live by, and we should focus on the cultivation of those traits. We cannot control whether a deal falls through, a computer crashes, or a helpful colleague quits.

But we *can* control how we respond to these scenarios: if the deal falls through, we can take what we've learned and strike up another; if the computer crashes, we can grab a pen and paper while we wait for the repair person to arrive; if a helpful colleague quits, we can wish them well and suggest staying in touch. We can also control our work ethic, resolve, and attention to detail. The Stoic example shows us that if we have cultivated the proper personal characteristics then this will enable us to best meet the challenges of the day. The idea is to not look at the rising flood water but to put all our attention and effort into stacking sandbags around the house.

Research supports Stoic tenets. A 2021 study linked Stoicism to mental health improvements, sorting 45 "high worriers" into three groups, two of which were devoted to Stoic training (one exclusively, the other as part of a combined approach). The training, lasting about 20 minutes daily, consisted first of reading routine Stoic passages and drafting written responses to them, then of providing "answers to the three core Stoic practices: predicting misfortune, examining judgments and completing a daily assessment."[12] Participants who had undergone the Stoic training exclusively self-reported

18% less ruminating, and the relationship between Stoic training, anxiety relief, and "positive affect" appeared to fuel emotional well-being.[13] Therefore, Stoicism remains useful today.

Action steps

The Cynics remind us not to waste time or energy on frivolities. What matters is not on the surface but in the deeper aspects of life. Do not worry about what your friends or co-workers wear, or even whether they flout convention (if they do). Instead, focus on what they have to say and share. Cynics equally remind us not to put on a face like we have it all together without cultivating our soul to match the virtue we want to convey to others.

In the Megarians, we see a focus on precision. Their concern with precision led to the formulation of dialectic or dialogue as an art. This amounts to an emphasis on discussions with other people through questions and answers. By pursuing questions and answers, we are able to guide our expectations about where the conversation is headed.

The philosophy of the Cyrenaics is centered on pleasure, especially the life-affirming kind. Their idea is to make use of what is within our immediate surroundings. It is easy to gripe about your new co-worker, but instead, you should appreciate your good boss. Similarly, yearning for a new Mercedes prevents you from enjoying the fuel economy and reliability of your affordable car in the present.

The Academic Skeptics took from Socrates the lesson that everything we observe, both within and outside ourselves, should be examined from all possible angles. But to see all angles, one must open oneself to every possibility. The Skeptics realized that as soon as we come to hold a position on an issue, this will be enough to prejudice us against other viewpoints that may have something to offer us. There is no harm in hearing someone out or there is no value in saying no to an offer before you can hear what it is about.

The Stoics remind us, in a similar way to the Cynics, to focus on the internal aspects of our self-development. Many more things in our daily personal and business lives are out of our control than in our control. But it is only through the cultivation of our personal character that we are able to face the situations that we regularly find ourselves in. It is not easy to let go of things out of our control such as natural disasters or unforeseeable tragedies. In fact, if the circumstances are personal, this may be more of a process than a single resolution. However, letting go of the uncontrollable saves many people's sanity and allows them the perspective of living a life relatively *in* control because that's where their focus is. That's how Stoics kept their sangfroid.

By surveying the various Socratic schools we have seen a common theme arise. Each school has taken a distinct element from Socrates' philosophy and applied it to their own lives in a very practical way. Much like a successful coach, Socrates was influential in inspiring many other students of philosophy. His charisma and personality were a force of nature in person, and this dynamism helps to explain why he inspired so many different philosophies after his death. It also highlights an idea Socrates himself advocated, that the spoken word is superior to the written words in several key ways, which we will investigate in the next chapter.

Chapter summary

- The example of the Cynics encourages us to always focus on the deeper aspects of life, not what is merely superficial.
- The Megarians emphasized precision and careful analysis achieved through in-depth discussions with others that followed a question-and-answer format; this collaborative effort worked toward a common goal.
- Aristippus and the Cyrenaic school help us realize that in whatever situation we find delight and appreciation in whatever circumstances we are in, because there is always some enjoyment to be found if we look hard enough. This does not, however, mean seeking pleasure through artificial means or to an inappropriate degree.
- The Academic Skeptics valued and developed the investigative curiosity of Socrates and promoted the lesson that to be open to

knowledge means to look into all sides and angles of an issue, reserving judgment until after we have seen all the information.
- The Stoics admired Socrates' pursuit of virtue and focus on the development of character instead of things out of his control, enabling him —and the rest of us who follow his example—to ably take on the challenges of work and family.

4

THE MAN WHO SHUNNED WRITING
WHY SOCRATES PREFERRED SPEECH OVER WRITING AND HOW YOU CAN ADOPT THE SECRETS OF SOCRATES' CONVERSATIONAL POWER

Have you ever called a large business hoping to talk over some complication concerning a product or service, only to be stuck with an automated phone system? In this situation, we may come to the realization that we have taken humans for granted. In particular, it is frustrating to have our customary back-and-forth conversations just taken away from us. We want to talk and be heard, and in order for that to happen, we have to be with other human beings.

The Socratic dialogues are full of this face-to-face interaction. In a general sense, this is the entirety of what Socrates was all about—talking with others. In Plato, Xenophon, and Aristophanes, we see Socrates discussing, asking, arguing, answering, probing, joking, defending, and sharing, all in the context of dialogue with others. Socratic life is about conversation and that means it is about other people.

Socrates was not a fan of monologues and long speeches. Instead, he focused on the give-and-take inherent in discussion, writing nothing down.

Whether his shyness at the stylus was a deliberate choice or antiquity's failure to preserve extant text from him is unanswerable. But one thing we can say for certain is that Socrates preferred the oral discussion over that of written texts, the latter of which he seemed to eschew on principle. Remember, this is not the same thing as saying that written language has no value for Socrates, but only that he saw in speech a number of advantages. In fact, as we will see later, there are ways to make written language work just as well as spoken.

One shocking conclusion that Socrates seems to lead us toward is the limitation of all language, spoken or not. While we aim at clarity in speech, there is something elusive about language that always escapes absolute precision. This is why discussions are an incessant back-and-forth between speakers. Clarification never ends. Details can always be added. New misunderstandings always arise.

Speech vs. writing

Socrates' praise of oral communication and critique of writing as an alternative can be found in the "Phaedrus."[1] There, Socrates insisted that good speech could only occur in one who understood "the real nature of things," both similarity and difference, and possessed the ability to be able to persuade someone by such a gradual degree that they were unaware of it. In writing, the speechmaker needed to be familiar with not only the soul but also its many types, so they know how to address any person based on observation of the way they conduct themselves. The speechmaker needed to know just what buttons to press in order to reach them—along with any other person he had to persuade over the course of a lifetime.

"When he has acquired all this," Socrates declared, "and has added thereto a knowledge of the times for speaking and for keeping silence, and has also distinguished the favorable occasions for brief speech or pitiful speech or intensity and all the classes of speech which he has learned, then, and not till then, will his art be fully and completely finished."[1]

Next Socrates turned more fully to writing, sharing an Egyptian myth in which Thoth touted his new invention–letters–as "an elixir of memory and wisdom." The god-king Thamus claimed in response that having written references would undercut memory because people would not be using it and that reading a written account explaining how to do something without somebody also directing them how to do it. The final nail in the coffin for Socrates is that you can't ask questions of a written work.

Writing was a new medium then, and Socrates had his suspicions regarding it. Nonetheless, he admitted, it *could* be done well if coming from "the mind of the learner" who possessed the same keen instinct of when to speak up and when to step back as the skilled speechmaker described above. But even then, writing served little value except as a reminder.

A writer, Socrates concluded, must "arrange and adorn his discourse accordingly, offering to the complex soul elaborate and harmonious discourses, and simple talks to the simple soul."[1] Until he does, he can neither instruct nor persuade.

Does writing undercut memory?

A text has everything you need "stored" inside itself, so you do not need to remember or retain the information in the text because you can simply return to it whenever you want to reference it. However, Socrates failed to point out that regardless of whether or not you *need* to memorize a text, you eventually *will* memorize it if you keep going back to it—fewer times if you read intently.

Consider a recipe you make. Every time you make the recipe you have to look up the recipe... at first. On Socrates' analysis, you do not know how to make the recipe. You are entirely dependent on the words set before you. But the experience of active reading plus reinforcement through actions *directed* by the reading will cement more and more of that recipe in your mind, so if you lose the recipe, you aren't out of luck.

The written word: dead or alive?

You may think of social media posts as impersonal, directed to no one in particular, but take a closer look at the language used. Is it formal? Modern? How long are the sentences? Any exclamation points? Typically, the person who posts is looking for a specific type of person to respond. With these questions, you can track this often subconscious intention behind a post and whom it targets. A new parent might vent about parenthood struggles to attract advice (and some much-needed sympathy) from those who have been through it before. Similarly, someone experiencing a breakup may post something negative about their ex in order to encourage a rash and poorly advised bout of public trash talk with some friends. In both of these cases, personal issues are broadcast widely but still target a more specific readership—as with books.

Socrates understood writing as unresponsive to argument or individual tastes: in a word, flat. Remember from previous chapters that he loved to converse with people from every walk of life on a wide variety of subjects. When you read the different dialogues, you begin to appreciate how varied these conversations can become, depending on just who Socrates is talking with. But back then, written texts tended not to be individualized to the reader's taste the way that speech is addressed to an individual, which is perhaps why he stressed the importance of personal tailoring in both speech and writing as seen above. Nowadays, however, you can't get anything published without knowing which market you want to sell it to. As the population and literacy rate swelled, options increased. A quick Google search today reveals a multitude of books sorted by genre and age group, among other factors. This variety and level of personal tailoring simply didn't exist in Socrates' time.

Considered permanent and unchangeable by Socrates, written text is still encapsulated in the human perspective. Have you ever returned to a book you read ten or twenty years ago and swore you remembered it differently? Our surroundings influence *how* we read, and our surroundings change. We drum up personal connections in addition to the personal connections offered in the actual text, drawing us out of our hardened shells of individual experience. Although they cannot physically speak, books can reach us in much the same way a human can. (After all, humans wrote the books!)

According to Socrates, speech can almost always elaborate and clarify, but written text can't. He compared written language to a painting of a smart-looking fellow. You come up and ask him several questions, to which he "preserve[s] a solemn silence."[1] Writing, he claimed, is just like this. The written text can give you nothing new but repeats the same things over and over again like a town crier yelling the same news. It needs its "parent," that is, whoever the author of the text is, to defend it if someone asks a question of the text or offers a criticism of it.

This is the essence of Socrates' distinction between written and spoken language: written language is not dynamic. It cannot respond to an individual's needs, it cannot expand or clarify what it means, and most importantly, it cannot teach because of these limitations.

But, as seen above, books can absolutely meet people's needs. Furthermore, a modern reader might point out the existence of editor footnotes to expand or clarify. Socrates might have counterargued that footnotes that were added later existed outside the original text and didn't count. However, written footnotes on a primary text are, apart from format, exactly identical to dialogue.

Written texts promote dialogue through discussion, either with another person, the work itself, or both. The best books lead to lively conversation, just as the best speeches inspire you to dive for your books for a deeper take, their symbiosis pushing you to strike a balance between formats—you need to have had your fill of one to appreciate the refreshing novelty of the other.

In the right circumstances, written words can have the dynamic ability to personally address someone, adapt to their understanding, and even teach a lesson or two. They also provide more time and space needed to digest philosophy's profundities, making for richer insight during a faster-paced spoken discussion that might otherwise have been missed. These upsides extend even to texts or emails that can be revised in a fine-tuned approach to better reach audiences and allow for the back-and-forth of a written (or typed) exchange.

However, two important qualifications need to be made. One is that in shooting off an email or sending a text, you have to be ever-responsive. You cannot send an email and then not follow up. This means that you have to answer any questions you may receive in reply, and confirm that the recipient understood what you meant in the email in the first place.

The other aspect you have to keep in mind is that humans are social animals (thank you, Aristotle). Speaking is something that comes naturally, easily, to people. Writing can take a little more time and forethought. There is also a larger possibility that the work will be misunderstood if the reader can't pinpoint the tone of voice. (Tone also comes through in writing, but usually not as strong.) But instead of viewing reading as inferior, it may be more prudent to adjust our expectations when switching between spoken and written conversation.

Socrates pointed us toward the various benefits of speech, which we try to incorporate even into our written language. In composing text we should anticipate questions and possible clarifications that need to take place and have an openness to more dialogue, which entails answering and asking more questions.

When it comes to questions, we have seen in <u>Chapter 1</u> that Socrates associates learning with dialogue, and that means face-to-face interaction. Importantly, speech is the kind of communication best suited for learning. During the recent Covid lockdowns, one lesson about childhood learning became clear: Children learn best during face-to-face learning. A 2022 study found that children and young adults alike were able to open a puzzle box fastest when watching it demonstrated from a 180° angle, or face-to-face, even though it was supposed to be more challenging than opening the box from a 0° over-the-shoulder angle. "A shared visual perspective increased imitation, but a shared mental perspective promoted goal achievement and the social transmission of innovation," the study concluded.[2]

Tying this into the previous lesson about the dynamic nature of speech, we see that learning is easier with face-to-face speakers because it is dynamic. It can be adjusted to the abilities, concerns, shortcomings, and development of the learner more fluidly than text.

Questions and answers teach in a way that other less hands-on methods cannot. They give us precision by eliminating possible misunderstandings. Imagine all the confusion that is saved if you ask whether "bi-weekly meetings" means every two weeks or twice a week.

If speech is effective, it is because it is dynamic. Socrates spent decades talking with people in public places and wrote almost nothing. Communication should aim at the dynamic aspect which he noticed thousands of years ago, for dialogue with others—be it written or spoken—is the fastest way to grow.

We should keep in mind when thinking about Socrates' advocacy for speech that he was in fact consistent, which may have served him but not so much the rest of us who only know him through *written* works that feature him. Whether it is Plato or Aristophanes, the records we have of Socrates' words were recorded by someone else, not the philosopher himself. The texts we have are all based on Socrates' circle, a vibrant community of discussion and social interaction. Xenophon and Plato both take pains to recreate the Socratic community through text, with vigorous debate and dynamic interaction which can be represented in a written format very effectively. But for Socrates, the meat of the argument lay in person-to-person discussion.

Action steps

Speech is never for its own sake but for yourself and whomever you are talking to. Furthermore, the point of all language is communication: to get a message from you to the other person in the best way. What you need to do is to mobilize all speech in a way that you get the most out of it. Take a leaf out of the "Phaedrus" and tailor your words to your audience, keeping in mind the many different types of soul and speech Socrates mentioned. Adjust for individual desires, experience, and understanding, being sure to consider your conversation partner as a person and not a mere intellectual tool. In fact, the very next time you talk to someone, take note of one instinct you have in this person's company. If they're going through a stressful time, do you avoid mentioning certain topics you know will upset them? On the contrary, does good news spill out of you when your friends are also happy? Hang onto whatever instinct you notice until after the conversation ends, and then consider whether you use this instinct in communicating with other people. Can you read people's wants and needs as successfully as Socrates did (or at least try)?

Keep in mind that you have to say things differently to your boss as compared to a co-worker, even if you are in essence saying the same thing. The formal setting of a business meeting is not the same as that of a family dinner. No matter where the discussion took place, though, Socrates held his speakers in rapt attention with his charismatic personality, and that meant he sought to understand them as individuals to whom he could customize his speech.

It's okay if tailoring to others' needs doesn't come naturally to you—or even if you go the other direction and only think about accommodating the other person. All it takes is a little practice! Most people are better at either talking or listening, but conversation is a two-part process. Working on your weaker skill is a great way to increase your social aptitude.

Speaking and listening are usually considered separately, as a 2010 study noted, but an fMRI revealed that two people engaged in intent conversation showed brain activity that was "spatially and temporally coupled" after a slight lag to accommodate the gap between hearing and understanding.[3] Researchers also found "anticipatory responses" at times in the striatum, medial, and dorsolateral prefrontal regions responsible for social processing; a high comprehension level accompanied this phenomenon, further proving the close involvement of the speaker to the listener in lively conversation.[4]

One important aspect of the dynamism of speech ties back to the first chapter of this book: any exchange that uses questions is better than one that does not. The mere presence of questions shows you are paying attention and that the conversation is going in a shared direction.

Chapter summary

- The act of writing has preserved Socrates in history, despite Socrates' preference for speech; writing allows the benefits of revision and pontification toward a deeper understanding.
- Speech should always adapt to the listener, addressing the individual within the limit of their understanding and appealing to their motivations and experience.
- Generally, the language we should all aspire to is dynamic, or responsive to a situation or a person, changing based on what people say to us and shifting to make clarity the main aim.
- Questions require the engagement of the speakers, bring forth clarity, and are an acknowledgment that language never ends. There is always room for more conversation.

5

ENOUGH IS ENOUGH

DISCOVER THE PERFECT BALANCE OF KNOWLEDGE WITH XENOPHON'S SOCRATIC GUIDE TO A FLOURISHING LEARNING JOURNEY

The absent-minded professor. The aloof intellectual unconcerned with anything but study. The egghead. The ivory tower. All of these are images that have stuck in culture, and often, these kinds of ideas are associated with philosophers in particular. One story about Thales, the first Greek philosopher, relates that while busy investigating the astronomical motions of the night sky, he fell into a muddy hole. After he fell, a woman chastised him for attempting to understand the sky when he couldn't even see what was at his feet.

This story, first recounted by Plato in the "Theaetetus,"[1] turned up in *Aesop's Fables* as "The Astrologer,"[2] although it doesn't exactly paint a flattering picture of the philosopher who set his time and effort to understanding often abstract subject matter. But this theoretical depiction of Thales does not capture the person of Socrates. In fact, Socrates was a very practical thinker, and as Aristotle notes, he was the first to bring philosophy down from the heavens to everyday concerns. We have seen previously that Socrates was a courageous soldier, an action-oriented occupation very much engaged with the more difficult aspects of life.

In this chapter, we will explore several different ways in which Xenophon, a contemporary of Plato and also a disciple of Socrates, grants us insights into the practical, everyday, and profoundly useful Socrates. Xenophon's works spanned history, philosophy, and even several technical treatises on horses. He wrote four texts concerning the life of Socrates—the "Memorabilia," "Apology," "Economicus," and "Symposium"—illuminating a more mundane side to the philosopher than can be seen in Plato. Three of these turn up again later in this chapter.

Xenophon's "Memorabilia" and "Economicus"

Socrates was insistent on learning the particular fields of knowledge that his friends had expertise in, and he encouraged them to expand their knowledge to new and different areas. Yet the limits that he pushed them to had an entirely practical orientation. He only wanted them to possess so much knowledge in a given area that was useful to achieve a measurable goal.

"The delights of learning something good and excellent, and of studying some of the means whereby a man knows how to regulate his body well and manage his household successfully, to be useful to his friends and city and to defeat his enemies—knowledge that yields not only very great benefits but very great pleasures—these are the delights of the self-controlled; but the incontinent have no part in them," Socrates claimed enticingly in the "Memorabilia."[3] Incontinent, of course, denoted a person who could not control their appetite for knowledge acquisition.

Later on in the "Memorabilia," he wanted his students to learn geometry but not for the abstract mental gymnastics the discipline requires. Rather he wanted them to master only so much as would enable them to know how to measure and purchase land. This way, they could properly manage business and avoid being snookered in a bad deal.

Likewise, when it came to astronomy, he wanted them to master the field so that they could know the times, seasons, and meteorological conditions of the day. But he did not want them to go so far as determining the motion of the planets or the distance between different celestial bodies. Socrates could find no use or reason to attend to these further unnecessary details and, in fact, he thought that they could hinder the acquisition of beneficial things in life. This idea also appeared in the "Economicus:"

"If I first show you, with respect to houses, some who build useless ones for a great deal of money, and others who for much less build ones that have everything that's necessary—will I seem to display to you one of the works of household management?" Socrates analogized early in the—dialogue.[4] His discussion about household management centered on farming, the handling of money, and domestic life.

The emphasis that Socrates gave to different activities like agriculture and astronomy shows us that there is a practical limitation to knowledge. We can pursue many different forms of knowledge but we must set a limit on them. There is so much knowledge in the world (and available on the Internet) that we could spend our whole lives learning more and more about any given topic. Because we have so many possibilities of what we could pursue, Socrates establishes a natural limit on that knowledge, in that we should care about only what impacts our lives in an immediate and important sense.

<u>Good goals come in small packages</u>

This Socratic insight has two applications. The first is that it should remind us that there should be a limit even to whatever it is we spend most time on which, in most of our cases, is our daily job. There is always more to master, more to uncover, and different lessons to connect in any field; your chosen profession is not going to be an exception to this rule. But Socrates' exhortation on limiting knowledge acquisition to practical use is really quite simple if you remember the sufficient, less-expensive houses he described: You only need to know as much of your job as is necessary to perform it well.

There are endless rabbit holes, but when you go down them, you are sacrificing your time and effort on other things. Most often, this is time with family and loved ones, but it could equally well be time you are neglecting for self-development. This could be social time with friends, intellectual stimulation, or just earned relaxation. At any rate, there is a trade-off, and the point of diminishing returns for your time is when you already know enough to do your job well, and the further pursuit of knowledge takes away from enjoying other goods in your life. This insight can also apply to more than knowledge—almost any pursuit can be taken to excess, costing you valuable time and energy elsewhere.

The other equally important takeaway from Socrates is that knowledge should be connected to some kind of goal. Focusing on knowledge's practical application is intuitive and serves us well in the balance involved. However, it's worth noting that big-ticket, Nobel-worthy discoveries develop more often out of obsession—i.e., excessively contemplating projects even at home—than out of punching a time clock. Balance is good until it grows stale, boxing us into the goals we already have. What of the goals that are to arise from discovery?

Perhaps the best solution is to find the balance of balance itself—and know when to justify putting more time into something. By placing a fixed purpose on the knowledge we have, it establishes a stopping point. But some things are worth a little extra time. If we have to know Microsoft Excel only well enough to create basic accounting spreadsheets, there is little need to take additional classes or conduct further research on advanced techniques. But if we find the inspiration to check out other Microsoft programs and maybe earn certification in something adjacent, we'll grow in knowledge even if there's no demand for that knowledge set just yet. Thus, we can still generally take Socrates at his word while allowing for some indulgences in knowledge acquisition to reach crucial breakthroughs.

Socrates' emphasis on the practical can be explained in another way when we look into the question of wealth raised in the "Economicus," his discussion of household management centered on farming, the handling of money, and domestic life. In contemporary discussions, many people conclude that wealth is something we pursue for its own sake and that if there is a kind of knowledge we care about when it comes to wealth, it relates to the acquisition of knowledge. But this is not Socrates' emphasis. He instead focuses on the necessary knowledge one must possess in order to use the wealth of the household.

In the Socratic view, it is simply foolhardy to possess something like wealth without the intelligence of how to use it properly. Socrates brings up the surprising example of a man who pays for a prostitute and is subsequently ruined by her. If it's true that money is helpful, then how could it be that money can be used for something obviously so destructive?[4]

The answer is that wealth has to be guided by wisdom. Socrates takes aim at the human obsession with acquiring things simply for the sake of acquiring them, whether money, houses, cars, or new phones. Cleverly finding a way to come into possession of these kinds of goods is not the wisdom we should be after. Rather we should be even more concerned with the kind of wisdom whose importance cannot be fully recognized until after we have acquired the object of value.

Exercising wisdom in knowing functions

It turns out that in every facet of life, even when it comes to something as simple as owning an object, there is always going to be a need for wisdom in how to *use* the object. This is related to the lesson above from the "Memorabilia," that all our knowledge should be related to some practical goal. But the emphasis here is different: Everything we do and everything we possess will require a kind of knowledge to use it properly. Without this knowledge, the object is harmful, not helpful, a loss, not a gain.

Consider a smartphone. Many people eagerly await the release of the newest smartphone model each year, even saving for months to afford the technology. But then they engage in wasteful and destructive habits because they do not know how to use the phone. Some people might say the phone is simply a tool, a neutral device that can be used for good or bad, productive or non-productive purposes. But this is not the way Socrates views it. His overriding concern is whether or not you have the knowledge it takes to use the item in the right way. In his view, you should not be using the item at all unless you know how to use it correctly.

But how do you know how to use an object before acquiring it? How do you know if you *don't* know how to use it? You'll probably have to rely on another person's instruction, or the Internet's, to answer the former question. As for knowing when you don't know something, you'll first have to follow up on some hunches or feelings of self-doubt through research to find out what you don't know according to a 2015 study.[5] After asking yourself, others, or the Internet questions, you are better prepared to find a knowledge gap. Follow this up by figuring out *why* you have the knowledge gap and sharing your knowledge to fix the gap for others. Sharpen your mind by working out all of these details and you'll soon be able to better track what you don't know. Outside of yourself, you can also invest in some online classes and community building.[6]

Another episode in the "Economicus" supports Socrates' overall approach to pursuing life in the light of practical knowledge. Socrates starts off by telling us the great importance of order in life. He brings up a few examples. Imagine a chorus without order or an army where everyone gets to move or behave however they want when they are on the march. Would anyone think that this is good? He also points us toward the discipline of the rowers on a trireme who must all row forward or backward at the exact same time.[4] Similarly, imagine someone who puts all their food into the same container. All these examples, Socrates tells us, lack order. But order is not something that comes of itself. Order is something imposed on things by a person with knowledge of the purpose of those items and a view to using them. Order, in Socrates' explanation, is the arrangement of different things so we can use them in the best way.

Keeping things in order is a kind of wisdom. This is a wisdom that best knows how to make use of things, optimize their readiness, and bring together different parts into a whole. But all of this, it should be acknowledged, is always for the benefit of a human. Order is never for its own sake or to exert control over powerless subjects.

<u>Conversations about practical application</u>

In Xenophon's "Symposium," we see Socrates conversing with friends at a dinner party. Though they are taking their leisure, Socrates is still focused on the practical challenges of life. In one of the most memorable anecdotes, Xenophon Antisthenes asks why Socrates has not educated his own wife in all the household arts and knowledge as he advocates other husbands do. Socrates answers that it is similar to a horse trainer (like we saw in <u>Chapter 1</u>) who wishes to work with the most difficult horse of all, since if an obstinate animal can be trained, all other horses will be easy students by comparison.[7]

Despite the unflattering depiction of his wife, Socrates was focused on the practicalities of household affairs and the particular way his own wife had to be "approached." Modern readers alienated by this frank objectification can self-soothe with the reminder that Xenophon lived over two thousand years ago and Socrates' views on wives in no way reflect the reality of a world split roughly 50-50. We'll take only what is still applicable from his dialogues and chalk up the rest to (unfortunate) historical context.

A more positive aspect of Socrates' character which consistently shows up in Xenophon is his willingness to help others. He not only wants to help his friends but he also encourages them to help each other. When he is talking with his friends, Socrates tells them to share the knowledge that each of them is most proud of. Later, this shifts into a discussion of what each man is proud of, whether beauty, righteousness, or something else. As it turns out, Socrates will evaluate each of his friends by how much a particular ability can help others. In effect, he wants to determine whether these people should really be proud of their best quality.

Again, what we see from Socrates is a turn toward the practical. The particular way that Socrates conceives of the practical is very important and deserves a moment of our attention. As you know, Socrates was always spending time with others in conversation. In a way, this was the entirety of his life. Socrates recognized that other people, those closest to us, make up most of what is important in our lives. In other words, if there is something more practically concerned with our daily lives than people, it would be very hard to find. To be practically oriented to the people in our lives means finding those things that benefit them. These can be knowledge, objects, or our character traits. The activity of our life really is the activity we share among and with others.

Action steps

Write down the different types of knowledge you use in your daily life. This would include the various types of knowledge you use in the office or at home, as well as anything you do in your spare time, such as hobbies, sports, or volunteer work. Write each of these in a separate column by itself. Then next to them make two more columns. One column should be labeled "Goal of this knowledge" and the other "Have I attained this level of knowledge?" The purpose of this exercise is to clearly lay out whether you have adequate knowledge to be able to perform the task at hand. Write down what the "Goal of this knowledge" is for each item. For example, when it comes to working out, do you have adequate knowledge of how to get and stay in shape? This or something like it should be the goal. If you do have it, then write "yes" next to "Have I attained this level of knowledge?" These are the areas of knowledge where you have topped out.

The trouble with topping out is knowing when you have, as with the don't-know-what-you-don't-know conundrum. According to scholar Anders Ericsson, it takes about 10,000 hours to learn a skill. This is more of an average than a hard and fast rule—some reject it outright—and as learning changes the brain profoundly, there is no set timeline for skill mastery.[8] But looking at the nervous system might answer some of our questions. Synapses enable communication between neurons or nerve cells—interestingly, neurons form synapses in the cerebral cortex during late-phase motor skill learning, according to a

2004 study.[9] This is known as cortical synaptogenesis, and along with motor map reorganization (which oversees voluntary movement), it occurs in the second of two phases: The quick first part of learning and the slower second part.

A 2019 study builds on this, asserting that the synaptic plasticity displayed in late-phase learning might function "to permit a network of neurons to generate new patterns of activity."[10] This could account for altered neuron tuning abilities, cited in previous studies, that in turn change the way sensory neurons react to external stimuli.[11] All in all, learning is something about which we are still learning!

There's just one problem. Even if you have a sense of which stage of learning you're in, neural activity isn't exactly something you can track at home. Instead, if you feel you've topped out in a skill, compare your progress with people you know and use your best judgment. Think of when Socrates would say you are good—then don't spend any more time on it.

Another inventory you can take of your knowledge is to compare it with what you possess. Do you own things that you don't need? The way Socrates advises us to make this assessment is to ask whether we have the knowledge to use and maintain all we have. Do you have a library of French books but can't read French? Do you own a lot of clothes but can't fit into them? Do you own a second car but never drive it? Socrates tells us that we must know how to use something if we want to use it well. To use something well ought to be the only reason we own something. Get rid of these "useless" things that you don't use, don't know how to use, or are unwilling to learn how to use.

Remember the beginning of the chapter and the caricature of Thales as a carefree intellectual who fell into a well. It turns out that that characterization gets something centrally right about Socrates: He is always concerned about knowledge.

But what it misses is that he turns that knowledge into a practical end, as Socrates always has a practical mind. In the next chapter will see how Plato emphasizes a different aspect of Socrates, the theoretical and speculative side, without compromising the idea that practical matters still take precedence.

Chapter summary

- Socrates taught his students to learn only so much of a given field as was necessary for them to perform a given task effectively; to go beyond this level of adequacy is to miss out on time spent on other goods in life.
- We should take the lesson of limiting our knowledge only to what is practical with an occasional knowledge-seeking binge on topics we are passionate about.
- In order to possess things, we have to know how to use them and use them well, avoiding items we

don't know how to use. This applies to money, technology, or even pets.
- Friends are the most practical concerns we have; whatever actions we take and knowledge we cultivate should be to the benefit of our friends.

6

PLATO'S SOCRATES

HOW TO KNOW YOURSELF, WHAT WE SHOULD SHARE WITH OUR FRIENDS, AND WHY WE CAN FIND PEACE IF WE GET TO THE BOTTOM OF THINGS

Plato is Socrates' most famous student, and Socrates himself is almost certainly more famous than he would have been without Plato. That is because Plato made Socrates central to most of the dozens of philosophical dialogues he wrote—and most people who are familiar with Socrates have read one of these dialogues. Because Socrates has such a charismatic presence in Plato's dialogues, there is a so-called "Socratic Question."

This acknowledges the difficulty in separating the historical Socrates from the literary character of Socrates. But it also deals with the tricky question of peeling Socrates away from Plato, the author. For simplicity's sake, we can take for granted whatever Plato adds to Socrates' character, as we are, for the most part, dependent on Plato for what he tells us about Socrates. In this chapter, we will focus on Socrates as the theoretical philosopher, a man who looked into the obscure details of reality.

The question of causes in the "Phaedo"

In the dialogue "Phaedo," there is an intriguing section that Socrates refers to as his "second sailing." In it, he gives a kind of intellectual biography of his early philosopher days. "When I was young, Cebes, I was tremendously eager for the kind of wisdom which they call investigation of nature," Socrates stated. "I thought it was a glorious thing to know the causes of everything, why each thing comes into being and why it perishes and why it exists; and I was always unsettling myself with such questions as these: Do heat and cold, by a sort of fermentation, bring about the organization of animals, as some people say? Is it the blood, or air, or fire by which we think? Or is it none of these, and does the brain furnish the sensations of hearing and sight and smell, and do memory and opinion arise from these, and does knowledge come from memory and opinion in a state of rest?"[1]

Eventually, he gave up investigating physical phenomena amidst his dwindling ability to know the causes of things, forced to abandon beliefs about what he thought he knew before. (Hence his "second sailing.") This drew him to more abstract subjects. He even shares that he was unable to truly understand how it was that simple addition worked. He knew that two and two were four, but he could not explain how this came to be. The most promising answer he came across was that all the physical things he was trying to understand were to be best explained by the mind. The mind or intellect was the unifying force, the cause, of all the things he saw around him.

Of all the lessons we can learn from Socrates, some of the most difficult to understand are these insights that deal with purely intellectual topics. But Socrates grounds his intellectual activity by relating it directly to his experiences. So, for instance, we see there are some striking similarities in this intellectual biography with other aspects of Socrates we have already seen. Socrates' ignorance about physical matter spurred his investigations into other areas, like what we have seen in the opening chapters about how ignorance is the first step to knowledge.

But what is Socrates doing differently in this "Phaedo" dialogue apart from turning to more theoretical philosophy? The answer can be summed up in a single word: causes. Socrates began to seek out the causes of things, for by finding a cause, he believed he would be able to understand why something was the way it was. "If anyone wishes to find the cause of the generation or destruction or existence of a particular thing," he instructs, "he must find out what sort of existence, or passive state of any kind, or activity is best for it."[1] This entailed *examining* the best not only for its own sake but also to know what is inferior. Such an approach allowed people to better understand the causes of things they observed.

Understanding why a person was angry, why the car didn't start, why the client didn't like the proposal, or why the shoes weren't comfortable—all are examples of understanding the causes. And to understand a cause is to prevent a problem, solve it, and look into the whole chain from beginning to end about why something turned out the way it did.

For all of Socrates' practicality, his probing curiosity here shows another side of him. This desire to understand the causes of things does not merely satisfy the same deep curiosity within us; it is also an acknowledgment that knowledge has a beginning and an end.

The "Apology:" Finding peace with death

In the "Apology," one very looming possibility is the threat of death. Socrates' approach to death is to follow the alternatives he is facing. Given that there is such a fate as death, and we all must face it, there are two possibilities: Either it is a reunification with our loved ones during which, as a bonus, we also get to meet the illustrious and noble dead, or it is a complete respite from the troubles of this world. In the second option, death is like a sweet dream from which you never wake, the oblivion of never having to suffer again.[2] (More about his trial and execution will be covered in Chapter 8.)

Here we can take a moment to unpack the core of Socrates' approach. In this case, you may think that all those philosophical musings about death did nothing to prevent actual death. You would be right—but that was not the point. The aim of Socrates was to give rest to his soul and to alleviate his worry. Once Socrates analyzed the problem of death and discovered those two possibilities of immeasurable bliss or unaware oblivion, all that remained for him to do was imagine himself in either of these positions. Perhaps one option is preferable to the other, but either way, Socrates thought out what it would be like for him to be in that position and came to a somewhat definite conclusion. When he did so, all his anxiety about the future dissolved.

Socrates could find a similar case in our own situation. If you can imagine these two possibilities in the case of your own eventual death, how much easier is it to trace the possibilities of any other problem you face? Consider what you think the possibilities are, then imagine yourself in each one. Just this simple exercise is sufficient to alleviate anxiety because it lays out the different scenarios. Socrates recognized that there is a deep source of comfort in simply knowing what *could* happen. Think of a horror movie in which all of the anxiety and fear depend so much on the unknown—not knowing where the bad guy is, who will be the next victim, or who the allies are. When we are able to grab hold of the answers, like a multiple-choice question, it makes it much easier to deal with the question.

On the other hand, escaping fear of death may not be quite so simple even if you do believe in the soul. A 2022 study investigated fear of death through the lenses of numerous social variables, finding "a positive association between belief in the soul and fear of death."[3] Experimenters chalked up this surprising result to doubt experienced amidst belief. Since no one can be certain about the existence of the soul, virtually everyone has some level of doubt and, therefore, fear. Fear of death is also experienced by those wanting to preserve their bodies through cryonics, as well as those who know their loved ones are watching them suffer and feel anxiety over it. Younger people tend to fear death more out of knowing less and relative immaturity. It seems Socrates is the only one who doesn't fear death.

Thinking while drinking in the "Symposium"

On a lighter note, the "Symposium" is one of the most pleasing dialogues to read. A mix of humor, philosophy and speeches on love, and the discussion between friends at a drinking party offer insight into the character of Socrates. Near the height of the dialogue, it comes time for Socrates to take his own turn at giving a speech in praise of love. Socrates relates a story about ascending a ladder from earthly beauty to the form of Beauty: "Beginning from obvious beauties he must for the sake of that highest beauty be ever climbing aloft, as on the rungs of a ladder, from one to two, and from two to all beautiful bodies; from personal beauty he proceeds to beautiful observances, from observance to beautiful learning, and from learning at last to that particular study which is concerned with the beautiful itself and that alone."[4] Such poeticism accompanies most of this dialogue that targets theoretical philosophy.

But Socrates did not come by this theory himself. Instead, he learned about love from someone else, the priestess Diotima of Mantinea. Socrates is not shy about sharing this dependence on Diotima with the other symposiasts.

This kind of humility is not often found in today's culture. There are people who are all too eager to take credit for a thought. Among those who have learned something from another person, many are quick to hide it. Socrates, on the other hand, gives credit to his source even though it was a woman, a significant fact when the symposium was a male-only party. But why was Socrates so eager to share his source? The answer is that he was focused on the purpose of the knowledge.

The insight we gain from Socrates in the "Symposium" is that knowledge is to be shared. This is not only because knowledge is something beneficial but because friends and family are worthy of receiving benefits from us. When we realize that knowledge is to be shared rather than become a secret, we are free to give it to others. When we do *not* acknowledge this, we want the knowledge to be about us. We are less open to sharing, wanting to take credit for the idea, and when we do share our knowledge, it is not to spread the information but to impress and overwhelm. In summary, what we see of

Socrates in the "Symposium" is that the benefit of sharing knowledge with his friends overcomes all other considerations.

Sizing up Plato's three-part soul in the "Republic"

One of the more famous innovations we see in Plato's "Republic" is the introduction of the so-called tripartite soul. As the name implies, in Socrates' understanding, the soul has three parts. The particular way that Socrates argues for this distinction is rather ingenious, showing that different parts of us desire different things and that these desires sometimes fight against each other and sometimes unite for a shared cause.[5] In the previous section in which we looked at the "Symposium," we saw that Socrates focused on sharing knowledge with others. But this kind of knowledge in the "Republic" is different. Now we are talking about self-knowledge: the degree to which you understand what motivates you, how you think, and what your mind really thinks.

Perhaps helpful for tracking motivations is our capacity for desiring "good" (good food, good drinks, etc.). When we *want*, we tend to want the very best. When you think about your motivations, consider the ways in which your body and soul are pursuing the good. Is your stomach rumbling for brisket? Or a longtime favorite television show enticing you to rewatch it? You will need to be in tune with what your body and soul are telling you. If you're distracted by other people or activities, you may miss cues.

In Socrates' case, he saw a three-fold self consisting of the rational part, the spirited part concerned with anger, competition, and pride, and the appetitive part that desires food, drink, and sex. Whether you think this is a good understanding of the mind or soul, the important takeaway here is the self-examination Socrates had to perform on himself to arrive at this three-part division.

Many people have thought that Socrates' idea of the soul is bizarre, and that the supposition of three parts to the soul is entirely speculative and unnecessary. But here is precisely where we can begin to appreciate the theoretical side of Socrates. The function of theory is to explain something, and we explain for no other reason than to understand. The theory is justified by the adequacy of the explanation it can give.

When it comes to understanding your own self, do you have an adequate grasp of what pushes and repels you? What actually makes you get up in the morning to do your job? Is it money, fear, love of challenge, or something else? What makes you stay on track with diet and exercise and what causes you to stray? To answer these questions you have to assess your own outlook. This is what Socrates did, and it was no idle task just for the sake of theoretical speculation. Trying to form a complete picture of your unique psychology will always be impossible, but seeing the contours of your motivations and cares, and how they differ from each other, sets you up to understand yourself well enough to get the most out of your life.

Action steps

Have you ever tried to solve a problem at work? When you looked into it, was there so much information and so many different opinions about what was going on that you didn't know where to begin? This glut of information represents in a very palpable way all the possibilities of knowledge. We have already recognized that investigation can quickly spiral into endless questions and unlimited investigations. But Socrates had a process of utter simplification. One must seek out the cause of the problem. If a product didn't sell, there might be many potential reasons why customers didn't like it. If we can simplify this into one overarching cause (although this is not always possible), then most of the work is done already. To know the cause of something is to understand the central fact about it, and everything else cascades down from this knowledge. Once you know this piece of information, you will know everything relevant to the problem you are trying to solve.

Socrates used practical simplicity in his own life to solve problems by finding out the singular cause of things. In the case of his own death, he imagined the possibilities for what would happen. The benefit was that he stopped worrying about what would happen; he was at peace after making his future more familiar and definite. Yet an important distinction should be made about the way that Socrates uses this technique. He had no choice regarding his execution—that was already decided. Therefore, he was not going through this mental exercise to decide anything, but for his peace of mind, and that alone. On a smaller scale, we can use our imagination of the future in a similar way.

Imagine two or three smaller tasks that you do regularly and a larger, single goal you have set for some time in the next few months. What are the possible outcomes for all these activities, not just in terms of success or failure, but the specific ways these scenarios might play out? Can you envision multiple scenarios? Just going through this rehearsal will put your mind at ease because now you are familiar with the possibilities and if it is a problem in need of a solution, you will be in a better position to find it.

The Socrates we find in Plato is an intellectual gadfly, but he is full of insights into how to live. Our mind cannot simply be separated from how we live, but we should prioritize our mental outlook in guiding the life we do live. When we live a life seeking out causes or learning from our friends, we can simplify the task of understanding considerably. Because there are strong psychological elements to the human creature, Socrates advocates for having a strong knowledge of the self in order to live a good life. In the next chapter, we will see how others' perception of us affects how we see ourselves and how Socrates dealt with this challenge as a public figure.

Chapter summary

- The Socratic principle of attaining knowledge is simple though difficult to achieve in practice: Find the causes of things by examining the existence, state, and activity that is best for the things we observe.
- Socrates, the intellectual, solved problems by assessing the possible ways they could be resolved, and he imagined his future by comparing the different outcomes that could come to pass. This not only helps on a practical level but it gives us peace before the outcome is decided.
- Knowledge is not an individual game but a team sport, and getting knowledge from others requires humility, not just to gain knowledge but to give it *to* others as well.
- Another aspect of the Socratic approach is to know what motivates us by understanding our pursuit of the "good" in all we desire. Your motivations give passion to your everyday activities, and if you don't know the competing motivations at play in your own life, you will not know yourself.

7

HAVE YOU EVER BEEN THE BUTT OF THE JOKE?
SOCRATES ACCORDING TO ARISTOPHANES AND HOW TO IDENTIFY THE LINE BETWEEN SLANDER AND CONSTRUCTIVE CRITICISM

Butch Cassidy and the Sundance Kid, Gandhi, Lincoln, Malcolm X, Lawrence of Arabia. These are famous names we all know. But these are also the names of famous movies many of us have seen. Our perception of these famous people has been formed through the popular presentation of their lives on film. This is even the case if we have read books on the historical figures in question. There is something about the dramatic presentation of someone's life that directs our perception in a way no other medium can. Even though we give lip service to the distinction between fiction and fact, when it comes right down to it, seeing with our own eyes is an illusion too powerful to overcome. It is hard for some people to imagine these famous people as anything other than the portrayals given to them by an actor.

The power of the ancient stage possessed this same ability to influence opinion, masked though the performers were.

During Socrates' own time, he was quite familiar to many of his fellow citizens. He gained a reputation for talking to everyone he met, bombarding them with questions, a social interaction many felt was odd or otherwise off-putting. Socrates' fame during his own lifetime gave Aristophanes, a comedic dramatist in Athens, the opportunity to write a play about him. Because the play was a comedy, we should always be aware that the first goal was laughter and not necessarily accuracy. But we can take away several lessons from examining Aristophanes' play about Socrates, *The Clouds*.[1]

In *The Clouds*, we first meet Socrates suspended from a basket in the sky. There, Socrates is conducting a kind of philosophical experiment to understand the sun and the air. He is "walking in the air," exploring the air's similarity to thought, in an early allusion to airheads. In any case, we encounter lampooning of Socrates' philosophy as soon as he arrives on the scene.

Recall that in the last chapter, we discussed Socrates' "second sailing," his intellectual biography of turning from investigating material objects to discovering more abstract concepts like the mind. Apart from parody, this passage in *The Clouds* may very well be alluding to this known aspect of Socrates' past. Just as many philosophers before Socrates began by investigating the natural world, Aristophanes depicts Socrates as taking up the same task. This is not entirely inaccurate. It matches, without the humorous overlay, much of what is said in Plato's "Phaedo."

In the rest of *The Clouds*, we see a buffoonish Socrates come to life. He is compared to the sophists, a group of traveling rhetoricians who would teach students to speak for a fee, often on any subject whatsoever. Sophists felt a great deal of pride in taking the more difficult position for sport. This gave them a reputation as unscrupulous intellectual mercenaries. As the comedy unfolds, so does Socrates' reputation as a charlatan. In *The Clouds*, Socrates has his own school called The Thinkery, where he teaches his students to investigate ridiculous and often abstract theories. According to secondhand conversation in one scene, Socrates wished to determine how many times its foot-length a flea can jump. To accomplish this, he made shoes for fleas by heating up wax and then had the fleas step into the wax shoes. The same conversation informs us that Socrates gave a friend the lowdown on where gnats make their sounds from. It turns out that it's their anus instead of their mouth!

These different episodes Aristophanes relayed build into a parody, and it has the effect of trivializing Socrates and making him a buffoonish rather than knowledgeable character.

Distinguishing Aristophanes from Plato's portrayal

The difference between the Socrates of Plato and Aristophanes lies in the perspective each held of the man. Plato was a philosopher, while Aristophanes was a playwright. There are even Socratic dialogues written by other authors which have not survived antiquity. In other words, there are (or were) lots of Socrates out there in the world.

When it comes to your own, certainly less famous, circumstances there is still an important lesson to be gained from all the perspectives on Socrates. You have to focus on yourself and what you are trying to accomplish. People will always have their own interpretations of what you are—good, bad, or ugly. Sometimes their perspective on you will just be radically different than your self-conception. But you have to continue on with the task at hand. To pay too much attention to what others are saying about you often does little more than give their opinions legitimacy and tempt you to give them more attention. This is even true if what they are saying about you isn't all bad.

From what we have already seen in Plato and Xenophon, Socrates was a man who sought out the truth, perhaps in ways that came across as annoying to his fellow citizens. But modern science is on his side. A 2014 study used an fMRI to assess curiosity's role in memory,[2] discovering that curiosity drove up nucleus accumbens[3]—housing the dopaminergic reward circuit—as well as midbrain function. In other words, curiosity and the reward circuit act together to make information stick significantly better. While curiosity is annoying, it serves an important function.

Aristophanes' depiction of Socrates seemed to have stoked and inflamed public animosity against him. But in the final analysis, we can say that the fame of his philosophy spread throughout the world. His inquisitive nature is almost synonymous with the nature we attribute to the archetypical philosopher. If someone as capable and famous as Socrates can have his good reputation challenged, then every normal person, by comparison, should expect to be treated no differently. There will be misunderstandings of what we do, why we do it, and who we are.

When it comes right down to it, we have no control over what people think about us anyway. They may have insufficient information, biases, or other obstacles that prevent them from fully acknowledging the way we want to be understood. Sometimes, people might be too favorable in how they look at you—a good example would be your own parents who tend to think of you in positive (and subjective) terms.

Socrates and the science of persuasion

A continuous theme in *The Clouds* is the particular use of language Socrates and philosophers more generally used. The focus on detailed, precise language is not something that most people are drawn to in their everyday interactions. This fixation on precise language parallels one of the oldest negative reputations of philosophy, that it is wholly impractical and absorbed with unimportant things.

Near the end of the play this emphasis on words manifests with two personified characters representing Just and Unjust. They bicker and insult each other, but their purpose is clearly to convince the young Pheidippides to adopt the position they are promoting. Unjust says to Pheidippides, "Come hither, and leave him [Just] to rave." Just answers: "You shall howl, if you lay your hand on him."[1] Although Socrates is not directly in the scene, it is clear that Aristophanes has him in mind in his use of dialogue.

One of the most serious charges that Socrates faced at his trial was corrupting the youth. We see in *The Clouds* that words are perceived as the most powerful method of persuasion, and that philosophy's method of persuasion takes whatever it has at hand to make a point. This is why there is both a Just and an Unjust; these two personified characters are portrayed as two sides of the same enterprise, defeating the other side by convincing the target audience.

There are a handful of lessons here to be learned about communication. When someone perceives that you are trying to appeal to some art of persuasion, whether by philosophy or some other method, they immediately become resistant to whatever you are telling them. This can be as simple as telling someone you are going to lay down the facts.

Imagine someone at work sitting you down as you are trying to make a very difficult decision. He tells you he has all the facts and is going to share them with you. You would probably be resistant to hearing anything he has to share unless he says something to raise his credibility fast. When we try to persuade others, we think we must speak in a way familiar to them in their regular life. But this is condescension at best and loss of persuasive value at worst, as it turns out. While it can seem counterintuitive to talk to someone in technical language or give them an abstract argument, research indicates that the more you sound like you know what you're talking about, the more persuasive others will find you.

A 2022 study looked at social exchanges from Reddit's subreddit *r/ChangeMyView*, which is designed for people with deep-seated beliefs to request arguments against their views for them to consider.[4] Researchers analyzed posts Redditors found especially persuasive through Language Inquiry and Word Count categories on a hundred-point scale, and concluded that longer posts with more technical language, context, and overall difficulty actually scored higher for message persuasiveness. Showing your expertise is therefore a good idea, but never flaunt it.

Another way this phenomenon can be approached is to say that persuasion should bridge your expertise to the listener's need. In *The Clouds*, we see that when arguments are made, a common human reaction is to perceive these arguments as manipulative tools. In other words, we believe someone uses the Just or Unjust argument with the idea that either one can be deployed depending on which is more effective. This seems to be little more than opportunism for anyone watching and undercuts trust. Whether someone takes you as opportunistic and a mere sophist or as credible and persuasive often hinges on the depth of connection you can create with your listener. If you are too flashy or too insistent, your message will probably be ignored.

On the neurological side, a 2008 study of persuasion and brain function discovered that "a single exposure to a combination of an expert and an [endorsed] object leads to a long-lasting positive effect on memory for and attitude towards the object."[5] Researchers showed participants picture pairs of a celebrity and endorsed object, and if the participants thought celebrities were experts, they remembered them more. An fMRI and behavioral assessment revealed activity in the prefrontal and temporal cortices during successful persuasion, implying heightened executive function (self-regulatory and planning ability),[6] memory, and language processing skills.[7] Expertise increased favorability toward the object by 12% and raised object recognition odds by 10%.[5] If the findings of this study are linked to the study on memory shared earlier in the chapter, they indicate that both curiosity and persuasion (in *being* persuaded, anyway) boost memory. This should encourage us to seek knowledge and persuasion.

On distortions and multiple angles

It is difficult to determine the degree to which Aristophanes accurately depicted Socrates—and, conversely, the degree to which he was offering a serious critique (if at all). But with certain perspectives like that of Aristophanes, we run into danger when we try to convince others through arguments—especially when we are just trying to appear more clever than the other person. We should avoid trying to persuade others for self-serving purposes for the obvious reason that people can pick up on that vibe.

"Talking out of both sides of your mouth" is one way we describe an unprincipled person who is unappealingly unpersuasive. But there is also a desirable element hidden here. This is the idea that you should be able to understand both sides of an issue. If your company is deciding whether to spend the last of the marketing budget on a controversial campaign, you should be able to give the pros and the cons of the campaign. What happens if the company decides to go forward with the plan you were initially opposed to? Now you face the prospect of executing a campaign whose benefits you do not know! This is quite the problem. Not only does knowing all sides of an issue give you greater insight into your own position, including potential strengths and weaknesses, but the knowledge may actually come into use in a practical situation. In the marketing example above, among other things, simply knowing that upside to the marketing campaign would have given you a better head start on what to do and an appreciation for the benefits of a contrary position.

We have seen how popular depiction not only shaped the popular reception of Socrates but also how it was a reflection of the popular opinion of the philosopher in general. The way that others perceive us is always going to be diverse and inconsistent. Every person views us only in part and they are apt to misconstrue this partial knowledge they have. This was true for Socrates and it is true for us as well. We should expect distortion, as well as what often turns out to be negative perceptions of our actions and thoughts.

Action steps

We are all on a stage like the character Socrates in Aristophanes' play. We have a limited set of words and actions which some people see and others do not. Some people like what we say and do, others do not care at all, and others may even despise us.

In Socrates' case, he was certain in his own mind that he was doing what he ought to have been doing—performing under divine mandate, a claim that will be explored further in the next chapter. This is exactly how we should approach the fact that we are always "on stage" and being judged for our performance. If we have confidence we are pursuing the right things in life, we have absolutely no reason to worry if others are forming the wrong ideas about us (especially now that execution by hemlock is out). This is related to the idea that we should mind our own business, but it acknowledges that there are others with thoughts that are out of our control. In other words, even when we mind our own business, others will see fit to mind it as well.

Make a column of names of people you know who have formed wrong opinions of you at one time or another.

Then off to the right, draw a number of circular "bubbles." In these bubbles, you are going to write the rumors, falsehoods, or misinterpretations that others have made of you. When you have done this, draw lines from the list of names to the bubbles if that person said that negative thing about you. You might have several people saying the same negative thing, yet sometimes there might be only one person accusing you.

But now it comes to the moment of truth. Either these negative claims about you are true or not. Go through them one by one. If something is true, now it is out in the open and you have a chance to fix it. Perhaps the charge is that you are undependable. Make it a priority to be a rock of consistency and to show your dependability. On the other hand, if people say you are lazy, and you can list your activities and accomplishments from the last several months, then you can ignore the criticism. Pop that bubble—put an X through that negative and false accusation. You have no reason to ever contemplate that charge again.

This exercise will accomplish two main objectives. One is to get those rumors and accusations about you out into the clear, rather than as a set of whispering voices at the back of your head. Now you can face them. Some will be absurd, and some might have some merit. The other aspect is that you will be able to associate what you heard about yourself with specific people. The purpose is not to become angry or resentful toward them. Instead, the idea is to make visible to you that the perspectives about you come from people. Perspectives don't just shoot up like mushrooms out of the blue. They originate from people. If you don't know from whom something true or false about you originated, make up a name to put beside the bubble—for you can be sure that it was somebody.

In addition, there will be things others say about you of which you have no awareness. (This probably accounts for the majority of the claims, although of course, you wouldn't have listed these.) Whether or not you seek out this invisible category of feedback is up to you. Although, it's worth noting that Socrates didn't, and even if he had, he would likely have gone down the same way because he refused to stop practicing his philosophy. As this exercise illustrates, other people's opinions are what you make of them—so don't make too much of them!

Just as it is difficult to imagine those historical figures listed at the beginning of the chapter as anything other than the way an actor portrayed them, it is mightily difficult to escape from the reputations others have given to us through their own perceptions of what we are. In more dramatic cases, like Socrates, the difficulty lies in separating the stage from reality. But in our own lives rumors, praises, and even slander all form the "stage persona" which not only can influence others but even our own view of ourselves. In the next chapter, we will see how the different opinions circulating around Socrates led to his indictment and eventual death.

Chapter summary

- Our reputation or image comes from many sources, some good, some bad, not unlike the representation of a historical figure in a movie. Aristophanes portrayed Socrates as an aloof intellectual (and object of ridicule) investigating obscure aspects of the natural world.
- Despite the different opinions of those around us, we have to forge our character and focus on our own projects, as we have no control over how people construe us.
- Our ability to persuade relies on sharing our expertise and matching it to the listener's need; "dumbing ourselves down" may seem like a better strategy but is ultimately less persuasive and can come off condescending.
- We should have a good grasp on the pros and cons of our position, as well as that of any opposing position. This helps us to know our own perspective better and allows for a more knowledgeable viewpoint on the whole.

8

THE TRIAL OF SOCRATES

AN EXAMPLE OF UNFLINCHING PHILOSOPHY, UNYIELDING RESOLVE, AND UNSHAKEABLE INTEGRITY IN A WORLD OF ACCUSATIONS

Imagine you have been sentenced to death. But instead of having death inflicted on you, you have to be your own executioner. This was the eventual fate of Socrates—sentenced to death, and forced to down a drink of poison hemlock. It slowly numbed and paralyzed the philosopher until his heart and body stopped completely.

This death, far from being something frightening or even undesirable, was something Socrates apparently entirely embraced. But why did Socrates embrace death, and why was he killed? In this chapter, we will explore the different accounts of Socrates' trial and death, the charges he faced, and what reasons he gave for facing death the way he did.

Reconstructing the trial

Both Xenophon and Plato wrote an *Apology of Socrates*. In Greek, "apology" does not mean seeking forgiveness, but rather it is an answer to a set of accusations or, even more simply, a defense. When it comes to the charges against Socrates, Plato and Xenophon are in agreement. The accusations brought against Socrates were that he was corrupting the youth, introducing new gods, failing to recognize the old gods, and taking money for his schooling.

Of all the accusations, corrupting the youth is probably the one that sticks in most people's heads. This nebulous charge reflects the fact that Socrates, by his own admission, spent a lot of time with the young men of the city as they followed him around and mimicked his way of questioning.[1] In engaging Athens' youth, he cut an odd figure—at the time of his trial, he was 70 years old and had a reputation for eccentric and often tiresome conversations. It is not often that you see 70-year-olds and teenage boys spending their social time together if they are not related.

At any rate, there was a generally negative public perception of Socrates. In the previous chapter, we saw in Aristophanes' *Clouds* a buffoonish portrait of the philosopher that could have been either a reflection of that public sentiment or one of the contributory causes of it. In either case, it was curtains for Socrates.

Arguing to the end

In Plato's "Apology," the Socrates we get is not someone who is willing to budge an inch on his way of life. He addresses the jurors directly, and it is they who would determine his fate—anything from a fine to the death penalty was directly in their power. Socrates insisted that he would not forego his philosophical conversations with the citizens of Athens because this was his divine mandate.[1] This was his purpose in life, and to ignore it was to go directly against the gods. Given Socrates' religious belief, the seriousness of this mandate cannot be overstated. His conviction to philosophize held such force in his life that it boiled down to a simple matter of obedience or disobedience. He pulled no punches when he said, "Men of Athens, I respect and love you, but I shall obey the god rather than you, and while I live and am able to continue, I shall never give up philosophy or stop exhorting you and pointing out the truth to any one of you whom I may meet."[1]

In Athens, citizens from any walk of life could bring charges against each other instead of public prosecutors doing so, as in many modern states. In Socrates' case, we know that Meletus was the chief plaintiff. Set right before the trial in "Euthyphro," he is described as having "long hair and only a little beard,"[2] with Anytus and Lycon responsible for the legal charges. Meletus was the son of a poet, while Anytus was a politician of some significance in Athens, and little is known of Lycon beyond his name.[3] In the "Meno," Plato suggests that Anytus was a man of low moral character, in that he did not live up to the excellence of his father.[4] Interestingly each of these accusers is said to represent a certain contingent that could legitimately be said to have grievances with Socrates for one reason or another. Meletus represented the poets; Anytus, the craftsmen and politicians; and Lycon, the orators.[1] In dialogues such as *Ion*, concerning poetry, and *Gorgias*, dressing down the claims of oratory, Socrates offered serious philosophical critiques of these very professions.

But Socrates also knows that he is fighting against public opinion. This broader public opinion seems to have been informed by Aristophanes' *Clouds* since one of the very specific charges Socrates mentions was that he made the weaker argument stronger. This is one of the consistent themes of that comedy.

Accusations assessed

In addressing the more general charges, smuggled in, as it were, through public knowledge, Socrates denies two broad characterizations. One is that he was interested in what is above and below the earth (in a more literal sense than heaven and hell, targeting modern disciplines like meteorology and geology). This amounts to the Socrates seen in Aristophanes: an intellectual pursuing natural investigations. Socrates says he knows nothing about this knowledge of nature. A second charge he refutes is that he was a teacher for pay.[1] Whereas the first charge put him in the same class with pre-Socratic philosophers investigating the causes of the universe, this second accusation was to place him in league with the sophists, itinerant teachers who unscrupulously charged their students for teaching.

In Chapter 2, we have already seen how the Oracle at Delphi guided Socrates' search for wisdom in others and himself. This explanation was a large part of Socrates' self-defense: Not only does it show he had a divine mandate to go around philosophizing with his fellow citizens, but it also gives insight into his persistence in pursuing his calling.

The way that Socrates answers Meletus' charge that he was a corrupter of the youth has a few different elements. One is to say that Socrates has no incentive to corrupt the youth—for he has to live among them as his fellow citizens! Why would he make the city he has to live in worse? No one would willingly make his own city worse, Socrates prods the jurors to concede. On the other hand, if Socrates did make the youth worse unintentionally, then the proper course of action would not have been to drag him into court. Instead, Meletus should have corrected Socrates and taught him how to improve his fellow citizens, not corrupt them. In fact, the accusation is turned back on Meletus himself. If he knew how to make his fellow citizen Socrates better but did not, then Meletus is the corrupter.[1]

Remember that unlike in modern democracy, the Athens of Socrates' time had legal expectations around religious belief. So when Socrates was accused of impiety, the charge was two-fold. He refused to recognize the traditional gods and introduced gods of his own. Socrates refutes these two accusations by proving that he both teaches and believes in spirits, which Greeks apparently understood as being the children of gods. If he believes in a son of god, it is impossible he should not also believe in the god who is the father of the son of that god. As to introducing new gods, he appeals to the common conflation of different ideas among different philosophers. Socrates was supposedly saying that the sun is nothing more than a stone, but this was a view espoused by Anaxagoras, not Socrates.[1] Socrates seems to take this approach of proving religious identity as a continuation from the "Euthyphro," which indicates Socrates' knowledge of piety. (He even voices his intention to use this knowledge to power his defense.)[2]

Socrates claims a divine mandate to pursue philosophy with his fellow citizens, no doubt threatening the established orthodoxy and inviting harsher punishment in doing so. But he is adamant in continuing, likening his religious duty to a military post which he dares not abandon until they give him an order to stand down. Another famous metaphor he invokes is that he is the gadfly of Athens, spurring and provoking others to thought and action: "But you, perhaps, might be angry," he predicts, "like people awakened from a nap, and might slap me, as Anytus advises, and easily kill me; then you would pass the rest of your lives in slumber, unless God, in his care for you, should send someone else to sting you."[1]

Nevertheless, Socrates is convicted of the charges and Anytus proposes the death penalty as the punishment. Socrates offers a counterproposal, detailed below, reflecting the many ways he benefited the public. He contrasts this with the punishments he could be given, which are evils, such as being exiled or fined, even though he has no money to give.

The penalty is decided upon. Death will be Socrates' punishment. In times past, he claims his divine sign, a "prophetic monitor," would issue a warning omen to Socrates not to do something. He declares that throughout his speech he did not perceive his divine sign interceding. This he takes as firm evidence that death is not an evil, but it is either like a pleasant sleep into oblivion or it is a reunion with all the blessed dead.[1]

In Plato's recounting, the charges are shown to be largely without any real merit beyond the general animus some people had towards Socrates. Socrates gives a defiant defense of his philosophical activities. Not only does he refuse to stop practicing philosophy, but he gets a little cheeky when it comes to his proposed punishment. After an initial vote by the hundreds of jurors, Socrates offers up the alternative that the state should give him a stipend along with free meals at the public mess hall like Olympic victors, insisting that he does not deserve punishment! Thus he made the most of what little life he had remaining.

Jailbreak?

After the trial of Socrates, Plato wrote another short dialogue called "Crito."[5] In this dialogue, Socrates is in prison about a month after his guilty verdict and is visited by some friends. Crito was a wealthy man about the same age as Socrates, and earlier, before the death penalty was pronounced, was willing to pay Socrates' fine. Due to religious sensibilities, Socrates cannot be put to death until a certain ship returns on its journey to Delos. His friends want to spring Socrates from prison by bribing the guard and having him escape into exile.[5]

Whether we agree with his conclusion or not, it is here that Socrates' convictions are on full display. Socrates insists that his conduct was right, about which he was prosecuted, and also that the Athenians are right in keeping him in prison in accordance with the law. On the surface, this sounds like a contradiction. But Socrates adheres to the idea that it is Athens and her laws that account for everything he has had in his life. If he decides to go against the wishes of the citizens now, it disturbs the entire social structure which has allowed Socrates to flourish. What if everyone disobeys laws that are thought to be unlawful, unhelpful, or harmful? No society like this could exist.

In the end, Crito's supplications to Socrates are unsuccessful. He will stay in prison until he faces execution the next day.

A slow death

In the dialogue "Phaedo," which is dramatically set the next day, Socrates is still in prison, where he will engage in another philosophical discussion.[6] This time the discussion is not about life or death but about life after death. Along with his young companions Simmias and Cebes, Socrates goes through four distinct arguments for the immortality of the soul: the Opposites Argument, Theory of Recollection, Affinity Argument, and Final Argument.

Opposites states that, like sleeping and waking, death and life are opposites, and each is generated from the other. Next, Recollection asserts that ideas of the Forms are given to us before we are born. Affinity differentiates between visible and temporary and invisible and eternal things, ascribing the former qualities to the body and the latter to the soul. The Final Argument posits that Forms cause earthly particulars, all things partake in Forms, and the immortal soul partakes in Life and not Death because invisible, eternal opposites never change into the opposite state, being unchanging. The mortal body partakes in both. (While people *living* can die—and according to Socrates the dead can come back to life—the Forms of Life and Death cannot become the other.)

Recall that Socrates' two versions of death from the "Apology" were immortality and oblivion. Following his thread of logic, these opposite states of death—the particular, not the Form—can generate into one another, allowing for the intriguing possibility that both are true at different times or perhaps even for different people. That being said, given that death is arguably temporary and immortality is not, immortality is the lesser choice for keeping Socrates' argument intact. In fact, given his stance on life generating from death, he could feasibly have argued that either state of death is recallable into the next life and thus "provable" one way or the other. Thus, his theory on death in the "Apology" neatly fits into the more expansive treatment of life and death in the "Phaedo," making for some fascinating eventualities.

As with the "Apology," Socrates' words are met with skepticism in the "Phaedo." In the latter case, though, skepticism comes with eager investigation by friends worried about their own eventual death.

The final scene of Socrates' death is one of the most moving in all literature. After drinking the hemlock, Socrates feels his legs numbing first and lies down. Next, his abdomen starts to numb. He utters as his final words, "Crito, we owe a cock to Asclepius. Pay it and do not neglect it."[6] Asclepius was the god of healing. The common understanding is that Socrates was saying that death would be the cure for his life's troubles. The cock offered to Asclepius would then be a sacrifice thanking the god for curing Socrates of the malady of mortality.

Socrates' sangfroid in his final moments might just be justifiable by science, difficult as it is to prove. A 2022 study shows that researchers got their hands on a brain scan of a man dying from cardiac arrest; an EEG captured activity during the unexpected heart attack. Researchers observed a "surge in absolute gamma power after suppression of neuronal activity in both hemispheres, followed by a marked decrease after cardiac arrest;" alpha waves also decreased during this period.[7] A high-stress situation will force your brain to work faster, and gamma brain waves are known to be the fastest and occur in a deeply focused state.[8] Anyone who has experienced this will know that trauma tends to center your attention so you can't think about anything else in that moment. Alternatively, alpha waves typically occur during relaxation, so a decrease there makes sense.[9] "Given that cross-coupling between alpha and gamma activity is involved in cognitive processes and memory recall in healthy subjects," the study concluded, "it is intriguing to speculate that such activity could support a last 'recall of life' that may take place in the near-death state."[7] The function of this may be to bring closure and peace to the dying, helping them across the threshold.

We don't know what Socrates was feeling when he died, but he had a track record of calmness and good humor. When he assured his friends he was at peace, we can probably take him at his word.

Xenophon portrays some of the details of Socrates' trial in a way very similar to Plato's. However, on one issue, they take very different approaches. Plato, as we have just read, says that Socrates eagerly embraces death because death is no evil; it is either a cessation from toil or an everlasting paradise. But Xenophon says that Socrates' motivation for seemingly embracing death was that it served as a welcome escape from old age. "But now," he says, "if my years are prolonged, I know that the frailties of old age will inevitably be realized,—that my vision must be less perfect and my hearing less keen, that I shall be slower to learn and more forgetful of what I have learned. If I perceive my decay and take to complaining, how [...] could I any longer take pleasure in life?"[10]

We see that the anticipation that Socrates has toward death is different for Plato and Xenophon. In Plato, it was something more positive for Socrates—the active participation in a heaven-like existence or oblivion. In Xenophon, the emphasis is more on what Socrates is going to avoid—the oppression which decrepit age brings. Interestingly enough, neither Plato nor Xenophon records these motivations of Socrates which the other mentions.

What comes next?

The aftermath of Socrates' death is one of the most consequential individual deaths in the history of the West. Socrates has often been viewed as a philosophical martyr, a man who died for his convictions. The impact of Socrates' dramatic fate was so strong that it set Plato off on his own philosophical career as a young man of 28. Most of Plato's dialogues feature Socrates as the main character. At the end of the "Apology," Socrates might even have Plato in mind when he says that his death will be the seed for future students. These students, he predicts, will come and rebuke the citizens for their unjust activities, presumably among them the condemnation of Socrates.[1]

Many years later, Aristotle was in trouble with the law courts of Athens. But instead of reporting to the charges, he fled Athens for a time, claiming as his justification he would not let Athens sin twice.[11] By this, he meant that the unjust execution of Socrates was enough of a historical blight, and Aristotle did not want to add to the list.

Socrates' two most famous sayings are probably, "I know that I know nothing," which we have already discussed in Chapter 2, but also the yet more salient, "The unexamined life is not worth living." Both these sentiments are expressed in Plato's "Apology,"[1] although the former is not verbatim. That should be no surprise because when push comes to shove, the true measure of someone's convictions is challenged by the reality of death. If you can uphold your principles in the face of death, you must really believe in them. There is the sense that Socrates is a man of commitment and integrity, and this matters even if we disagree with what he thinks. Of course, after the death of Socrates, Plato would go on to found the Academy in Athens, a philosophical school dedicated to the life of the mind and the kind of examined life worth living.[12]

Influential philosopher Georg Hedel gave a series of lectures on Socrates in *Lectures on the History of Philosophy*.[13] Like the overarching principle of synthesis that he saw working itself over history, he saw in Socrates and Athens two sides which in themselves were irreconcilable. Athens represented the side of the majority and tradition. These were the laws and moral code which are developed and interwoven into a given culture. On the other side, in Hegel's assessment, Socrates was the vanguard of a new type of ethics, the ethics of the self. This was not so much a turn to subjectivity as a reorientation of decision-making, from corporate to individual responsibility.

In light of Socrates' modern reputation as a martyr, Hegel offers a radical conclusion that Athens was, in some sense, justified in her condemnation and execution of Socrates. He saw both sides as right, similar to what the philosopher himself claimed in the "Crito": Just as Socrates had the right to philosophize in private settings —especially where he "expressed the higher principle of mind with consciousness"—so did the State have the right to prosecute what it deemed wrongful or dangerous behavior. (Socrates' claim of acting by divine mandate was likely considered subversive.) "A reaction had to take place, for the principle of the Greek world could not yet bear the principle of subjective reflection," Hegel concluded. "The Athenian people were thus, not only justified, but also bound to react against it according to their law, for they regarded this principle as a crime."[13]

In *The Birth of Tragedy*, Friedrich Nietzsche argues that Socrates marks the *death* of tragedy. Nietzsche pulled no punches portraying Socrates as someone who promotes rationality above all else and also pits death against life, preferring the pie-in-the-sky afterlife instead of life in the here and now. "What a pity one has not been so fortunate as to find the cup of hemlock with which such an affair could be disposed of without ado: for all the poison which envy, calumny, and rankling resentment engendered within themselves have not sufficed to destroy that self-sufficient grandeur!" the modern philosopher seethed against Socratic and Greek influence, certain that all cultures at times were desperate to get out from under their thumb.[14]

In art, there are some beautiful pieces that have been inspired by Socrates' death. The Italian artist Antonio Canova (1790-1792) took inspiration from the "Apology" and "Phaedo" in creating three bas-reliefs. They depict Socrates speaking to the jury, the moment he is about to drink the hemlock, and after death when Crito is gently closing his eyes and mouth. The stark white reliefs depict little more than the essential background details in order to foreground the action sequences centered on Socrates.

The Death Of Socrates Painting

Probably the most famous piece of art concerning Socrates's fate is *The Death of Socrates* pictured above, painted by the Frenchman Jacques Louis David in 1787. In the painting, Socrates is reclining on a bed in his prison chamber while surrounded by friends who are either despondently turning away or totally focused on Socrates' next move. Socrates looks at one of his friends, perhaps Crito, while pointing his left index finger upwards. With his right hand, he reaches for the cup mindlessly. Socrates' confidence, strength of body, and height (he is taller than everyone else, though on a bed), in addition to the luminous white image he presents in the center of the painting, give the impression that he is indeed off to a better fate.

It really is hard to imagine putting our lives on the line with such conviction that we are willing to die. Do you have a set of principles for which you are willing to die? A list of tasks you wish to accomplish? Most importantly, from the Socratic standpoint, do you have a set of principles worth living by? Socrates' trial and death were representative of a commitment he lived his whole life. This consistency of character seen in his death is a reflection of his commitments, his so-called "theoretical thoughts" which have a real-world impact. We will look at more of these world-changing beliefs in the next chapter on Socrates' main teachings.

Action steps

Let's hone in on some of the tasks you want to accomplish before you die. We usually call this a bucket list. A 2018 study that surveyed 3,056 participants on such lists unearthed six common desires: travel, meeting personal goals, experiencing milestones, spending time with loved ones, reaching financial stability, and considering daring activities.[15] Whether any or all of these speak to you, you'll soon get a chance to write down your own goals—but we won't stop there.

Grab a pen and two sheets of paper. Write "Life Accomplishment Wish List" at the top of the first page (or "Bucket List" if you're more traditional). Acting as though you are a participant in the study, write down six things you would like to accomplish in your life. They can be as similar or different from the above categories as you want, but the more detail you go into, the better. (*Where* do you want to travel? *Whom* do you want to spend time with?) When your list is complete, turn to the second sheet of paper.

At the top of the second sheet, write "Completed Life Accomplishments." Fill in six accomplishments you have already achieved, again being as specific as possible. Anything you've done that you or others are proud of can be added. Additionally, if you've made some progress on unachieved long-term goals related to your first list, write it down.

Lay down the two lists side-by-side, the wish list on the left. Take note of any common themes and, ending with the completed list, pat yourself on the back for everything you've been able to achieve so far… and for examining your life to make Socrates proud.

Imagine you have been sentenced to death, damned to drink poison. You are seventy years old. Don't think about what you haven't done, just what you have. Still, if fear or dissatisfaction flutter through you in place of Socrates' calm, perhaps you can appreciate how difficult it is to keep your head when about to be executed.

Chapter summary

- Socrates faced many charges at Athens, including corrupting the youth, not recognizing other gods, taking money for teaching, and pursuing subversive scientific investigations.
- Socrates deftly defended his own innocence by arguing that he could not have corrupted the youth, for this would involve actively making the citizens he lived with worse.
- In the "Crito," Socrates upholds the rule of law by refusing to escape his execution.
- As Socrates drinks the hemlock, he asks Crito to offer a cock to Asclepius, an acknowledgment to the god of healing that he was being healed of life's maladies.

- While in Plato, Socrates embraces death whether it means going to paradise or a dreamless sleep, the Socrates of Xenophon says that he does not wish to be subjected to the debilitating effects that old age has on the body.

9

SOCRATES' BLUEPRINT TO REAL HAPPINESS

HOW TO EMBRACE VIRTUE, BUILD HOLISTIC CHARACTER, GAIN INNER WEALTH, AND FIND JOY BEYOND THE EPHEMERAL

Everyone wants to flourish. But very few pursue lasting happiness, at least not in the capacity of philosophy. We often live in such a way that we make purchases and choose actions that may give us a sense of purpose and joy, which lasts for a little time and makes for a rare occasion. But someone who systematically plans for a life of flourishing, much less attains it, is rare. One of the things that absolutely set Socrates apart was his dedication to the pursuit of happiness. In Greek, the word "eudaimonia" is often translated as "happiness," but the type of happiness that Socrates is talking about is a lasting one. Therefore, "flourishing" is a closer choice. It means to be well-favored by a god or god-like figure. Unlike English, the Greek conception of happiness concerns an objective state of affairs; it does not refer merely to a subjective feeling or a mood when we think we are experiencing the best of life.

Flourishing and living well were the entirety of what Socrates' life was about. It is from this angle that we examine his main teachings, learning from Socrates as an example both in word and deed. Part of the reason is that Socrates himself, most famously in Plato's "Apology," denied that he was a teacher of anything. But this was an acknowledgment of his own ignorance, or as we might say, his own limitations. He also wanted to avoid the impression he was doling out advice as a mere mercenary, to whomever requested it. To truly learn from Socrates, we have to look to his life.

Savoring the ethical life

The first concept we will examine is the idea that flourishing is essentially bound up with virtue. For Socrates, this was not the idea that we tack on virtue to happiness in line with the very prevalent corporate principle that whatever we do, we must do it ethically. Socrates' conviction was that virtue leads to the good life and happiness is nothing other than the good life.

If we look closer at Socrates' idea, we see that life itself is an activity and, furthermore, that the one big activity of a life from birth to death is composed of many smaller activities. Because life is an activity, this means we are *doing* something. It also means *we are the moral agents* doing that something. The Socratic approach to life is that life is activity, and just like any activity, it is to be done well. If you are a doctor, you have a good bedside manner. If you are a businesswoman, you turn over a decent profit. So on and so forth for every job.

Doing something well is another way to explain the broader concept of virtue. The Greek word for virtue is *arete*, and this involves excellence of any kind. So the virtue of a knife is to be sharp while the virtue of a chair is to seat someone. Each type of thing has a virtue belonging uniquely to itself. This also includes mankind. The virtue of mankind is living well. In this type of understanding, living well cannot be achieved without virtue because it is nothing other than virtue. As Socrates says in the "Republic," "He who lives well is blessed and happy."[1]

Living well involves many factors, but it does not mean partaking in what some may call the "high life." Living well is not eating gourmet food or lying out on the deck of a yacht. It involves not being someone who is wicked and full of vice, on the one hand, and on the other, actively participating in activities that make the human being flourish. At first glance, this may look somewhat different than it did in Socrates' day, but as the adage goes, "the more things change, the more things stay the same." Virtue involves being honest in your business dealings. If you manipulate people, do things in a dishonest way, put money before everything else, or treat your co-workers unfairly or inhumanely—these are all disqualifications from flourishing in the Socratic sense. You may even have a mood of self-satisfaction, but emotional elation by itself does not mean you are flourishing. For Socrates, this amounts to self-deception. To be happy in life, you also have to be a good person.

On the flip side, you may be wondering about the benefits of living you-first. Socially-accommodating folks may take less time and thought for themselves, for example, and therefore seek it. This, too, is a valid approach, and a 2020 set of two studies that produced new scales for healthy selfishness shows that there are some benefits to living selfishly. These include, obviously, taking better care of yourself and being less preoccupied with the needs of others. Furthermore, healthy selfishness actually fosters "growth-oriented and intrinsically enjoyable reasons for helping others."[2] In other words, indulging your selfish desires means you get more out of altruistic temptations. (You do, however, want to avoid the "bad" selfishness known as pathological altruism, or overzealousness of good intentions that often produce bad circumstances, whenever possible.)

Another aspect of healthy selfishness is prioritizing those important to you. Positive relationships with loved ones help you flourish as seen in a 2010 study in which the interactions of 47 octogenarian couples were observed over eight days. Couples spent over 70% of their time awake with others and half of that time awake with spouses, claiming less pain on their daily reports while "moderately happy."[3] If the previously discussed study indicates controlled selfishness is good for us, then this one shows the similar benefits of moderate, stable happiness. Living virtuously and the more modern model of living for you and yours should exist in balance for your best chance at flourishing.

How many virtues are there?

Related to the theme that virtue is happiness, we can also look at Socrates' conviction that all virtue is one from the "Laches."[4] This is a strange idea, to be sure, but consider an analogy. Imagine there is a painter who claims to be quite excellent at his work. He can paint houses and flowers and people. But strangely enough, he cannot paint trees, animals, or the sky. It's not a matter of not wanting to; it's that when he attempts to do so, he paints a big mess instead of the object he was attempting to depict. If you think that this man is not a painter, or at least not a painter *in the full sense*, then you can begin to see what Socrates was getting at.

Socrates claimed that all virtues are one in that it was simply impossible to possess only one of the virtues. For the Greeks, the cardinal virtues were four: wisdom, temperance, courage, and justice, as Plato would claim in the "Republic."[5] To possess one of these virtues, you must possess all four. Why might this be? Because in order to be wise, you have to be temperate, courageous, and just. And in order to be courageous, you have to have the wisdom to act courageously only in the right situations and for the right reasons. In order to be temperate, you have the wisdom to apply your temperate activity in the right way and the courage to do so. In other words, the virtues are always overlapping one another. To try to possess one without the other is like having a hand without an arm—as soon as it is disconnected from the arm, the hand, as a detached object, ceases to function as a hand.

The Greek virtues are one case, and the most important for living well. But there are also virtues when it comes to the modern workplace. These kinds of virtues can be easily listed, such as being punctual, hardworking, cordial, diligent, quick to respond, and many others. Now, it may seem a little odd to us to think that all these workplace virtues go together. But let's look at a clearer case first. Imagine a mostly good worker: punctual, hardworking, cordial, and diligent. But he never answers his email or phone in a timely manner. Unless he works on this weakness, it will continue to undercut all of his strengths, even compromising his status as a "good worker." There is a bond of association between these different workplace virtues. It may seem unfair to those of us who aren't perfect, but thankfully you don't need to be perfect to sand down your rough spots and embody confidence and competence in the workplace.

What accounts for this unity of virtues? Why is it that when you see someone who is punctual, she also tends to be diligent? The general reason is that all these virtues belong to a person with a certain kind of character. Forming character takes a long time, but it also begins with the conviction of a mindset. Do you have what it takes when it comes to being a good worker and possessing workplace virtues? You have to *want* to be virtuous before you can be virtuous. This is the first step toward being an excellent worker or, for that matter, an excellent friend, son, father, mother, or sister.

There is another way in which the virtues are one. This is a recognition that the virtues are "sticky." In other words, good practice in one area leads to good practice in another. When you start getting to work on time, then you also start to become more focused on meeting deadlines. This makes sense, because getting to work on time is a kind of deadline. Being a hard worker leads to pursuing the other kinds of workplace virtues. When we say someone is a "good worker," what we mean is that their excellent actions at work are unified in a single person; we find it hard to separate their good qualities from each other. Granted, it can be done (think school or workplace evaluations). But when someone radiates good qualities, they tend to exist under the umbrella term of "good" and blur together until we take the time to examine and differentiate them.

We have seen in [Chapter 2](#) the importance of Socrates' own awareness of his ignorance. But there are also convictions that he held and demonstrated in the "Apology"—so we know that his claims of utter ignorance are not to be understood as categorically denying knowledge. In fact, there are some ideas he most certainly affirms. We can call these bedrock principles, convictions held with such earnestness that we will not give them up in the face of difficulties, or in Socrates' case, even upon the threat of death.

One of these principles is Socrates' abhorrence of the way people value what is trivial over what is essential.[6] This sounds rather obvious, but the main way Socrates wants this to be taken is to value the development of one's soul above all else. This means valuing the things that are valuable to the soul above those that are valuable to the body. In a practical application, this could be extended to many pursuits in our own lives. If we regularly spend many hours on the weekend detailing our car but neglecting a human relationship that needs repair, we must reassess why we are doing this. Socrates would say the relationship is worth far more than a shiny wax job and a spotless interior. Another example might be taking in pleasing entertainment at the expense of developing the mind. If you never devote time and energy to improving your mind but indulge in movies, video games, and other passive forms of distraction without pause, you may need some mental exercise.

Hammer or nail: Socrates on doing wrong

A last and very important Socratic principle is Socrates' idea about wrongdoing. This pairs well with his tenet of valuing what is virtuous and good for the soul. It goes without saying that he does not advocate wrongdoing, but in the dialogue "Gorgias" he goes a step further, asserting that it is worse doing injustice than having it done to you.[7] Today, there is resistance to this idea. People often reason that if they do wrong to others, at least they are in control of what is happening and have some power. But among Socrates' chief concerns is that doing wrong to others *is* in our control. That is, we can worry about someone else doing something to us, but that is not in our control. We can only control what we do to others.

For simplicity's sake, what we do to others can be considered good, bad, or neutral. However, from a cultural relativist standpoint, you may think something is bad that someone else deems good, and vice versa. Most people believe in a few absolute rules, like murder and stealing being bad—though self-defense and starving could justify it—but unless you plan on committing atrocities, your choices will likely fall in a gray area of subjectivity. Further complicating matters, something thought of as good now may be revealed many years later as being not so good. (Think Nazism—enough people thought it was good to vote for Hitler in 1933.)

With all this potential confusion, how do we accurately assess our actions? You can channel Socrates' ethics and simply try to do what is virtuous, although this is easier said than done. You can also take a utilitarian approach, such as maximizing good by pleasing as many people as possible. Another alternative to consider is a deontologist, "duty-based" approach that cautions against wronging anyone. To distinguish these, a utilitarian would justify killing one person to save a thousand, but a deontologist would likely refuse. Unless killing that person would create significant virtue (as in the case of a dictator responsible for genocide), the virtue ethicist would probably also refuse. In sum, ethics is far less straightforward than it might seem at first glance. The best thing you can do is choose an ethical approach that suits you and listen to your conscience. Be sure to get others' input once in a while, too, so you aren't living in an ethical vacuum.

Moving back to Socrates, we see how emphasis on the important aspects of life is the counterpart to this idea that it is better to be wronged than to do wrong. Both of these principles emphasize our agency or responsibility to do something. One principle recognizes our responsibility to do good, while the other recognizes the responsibility to refrain from doing bad: This marks the difference between positive and negative ethics.

Action steps

Flourishing was Socrates' entire reason for life. His teachings on happiness are visible in all he said and did. Consider the occasions when you have determined you were happy in the conventional sense of the word. How long did these occasions last? Did they go away quite rapidly, and what caused them to go away if so? Was it a momentary elation or a bad event? If it lasted, was it flourishing? Whether or not you know how it feels to flourish, there is ample reason to take Socrates' call to action in the pursuit of excellence.

Flourishing is not something that just happens to you, nor is it something that comes and goes. It reflects the consistent state of character of someone who regularly chooses the virtuous way of life. This was primarily in the ethical domain for Socrates, but we can also think of it in the workplace or our personal lives. Developing a consistent set of actions you perform as an employee, spouse, or friend will grant you contentment which will be much more permanent and satisfying than the passing moments of elation often associated with happiness.

When it comes to the virtues or excellent habits you are forming when it comes to being an employee, spouse, or friend, consider the most important traits. What are the five most important actions to fulfill your role in the most impactful way? It could be spending a certain amount of time with loved ones or accomplishing weekly tasks at your job under deadline without any reminders. List these typical three roles of spouse, employee, and friend, or substitute one of your own. List the five most important action steps you need to take, even if you have already taken some or all of them. Now assess them: Do you find that you are pursuing and achieving these five steps or not?

This is the heart of what Socrates was attempting to get at. Your relative level of achieving each one of the five will probably have some relationship to each of the others. This is both good news and bad. On the one hand, you are generally going to be only as good in each area as you are in the others, while on the other, as you improve in one you will find yourself improving in the others.

There is another self-examination that must be performed, not just in terms of what ought to be pursued but also as to what needs to be left behind. This means taking inventory of those activities that harm our development and hinder the five activities you listed above. These can be obvious, like an addiction or some other kind of vice, but may also mean a hobby that has tended to consume you at the expense of friendships, money, or other good things. (Note that many such things can go both ways and the above statement refers to *healthy* friendships and money pursuit.) Socrates' insight is not only to pursue those things that lead to our excellence, but to shun and flee those things that are ultimately harmful, be they small or great. The most important factor guiding our decision-making should be the development of our character toward excellence and the ultimate fulfillment of happiness.

Inspiringly, a 2019 study discovered flourishing even in those experiencing hardship. Researchers collected questionnaires from 51,156 American children, ranging from six to 17 in age, a significant amount of whom came from lower-income households, had special needs, or had other "adverse childhood experiences." Flourishing occurred across the board even in adversity at a whopping national rate of 40.3%, measured by an ad hoc three-item Child Flourishing Index that asked parents about their children's "interest and curiosity in learning new things, persistence in completing tasks, and capacity to regulate emotions."[8] The high index scores prove that flourishing can happen anywhere and at any time.

We have talked about some of the ways in which virtue relates to living well. The path of living well is nothing other than flourishing and the contentment it brings. If Socrates were interested in teaching us anything, he would perhaps impart a greater concern for our own happiness. This does not amount to merely wishful thinking. We must deliberatively strive to attain virtues while recognizing that those virtues are all interconnected. We seek to learn from the philosophy of Socrates this lesson, to cultivate our souls, excellences, virtues, and the eventual securing of our happiness.

Chapter summary

- Socrates sought flourishing, or a blessed life, through virtue and knowledge.
- Flourishing is closely associated with virtue, understood as excellence of every kind. To be happy, you have to be virtuous; to be virtuous, you have to be pursuing happiness.
- Virtue, or the collection of excellences a person may have, is one, meaning that in order to possess one good trait, you must possess them all. But don't despair: Good habits and skills are "sticky"—when you cultivate one, you cultivate all.

- Socrates reminds us to value what is important over what is less so—committing through time, energy, and money spent on things that are really important, like people, and not material objects.
- The most important issue in our lives is developing and caring for our souls because it is in our control to do good and refrain from evil, though many things remain outside our control.

10

WHO'S THE WISEST OF THEM ALL?

THE LEGACY OF THE GADFLY PHILOSOPHER AND HIS GIFT OF UNFLINCHING QUESTIONS FOR BOTH ANCIENT AND MODERN CRITICAL THINKERS

Few people have ever quite cared less for the opinions of others than Socrates. He was, above all else, guided by staying true to himself, the gods, and his divine sign. The opinions of the many, the great, or the powerful did not automatically garner obedience or respect. Yet despite this, Socrates is probably the most influential philosopher in terms of the opinions he has inspired in others by his tenacity of inquiry and the martyrdom of his trial and death.

We saw in Chapter 3 all the different kinds of Socratic schools that followed after Socrates' death. But his influence continued and continues to this day. Just as we saw earlier, there are many "Socrateses"—different people take away different things from this complex character.

Historically, there are two main categories of Socratic influence: his actions and his doctrines. The actions are in some ways much simpler because they tend to concern his trial and death exclusively, most commonly centering around the Socrates seen in Plato's "Apology." The doctrines are taken from the rest of the philosophical dialogues, many of which we have already discussed.

You may have noticed that Xenophon or Aristophanes aren't mentioned. That is because as time went on, the Socrates of Plato took center stage, and other reports of Socrates faded into the background, generally neglected in comparison to the charismatic Platonic Socrates. You may be surprised to learn that there were other Socratic dialogues not written by Plato or Xenophon. Now lost, they were apparently popular in Aristotle's time, and he makes several references to them. These Socratic logoi are another source of information on the philosopher and indicate that interest in Socrates did not fade after his death, it instead resulted in a cottage industry of these writings which gave additional light to his life.

In the Roman period, Socrates remained a hugely influential figure. For Cicero, who was closely associated with Plato's Academy, Socrates was a principled and wise philosopher. Seneca refers to Socrates as a sage, a man who has attained the exceedingly rare acquisition of wisdom.

But how is wisdom measured, and how does its value permeate society? A 2013 review of 31 articles exploring empirical definitions and subcategories for wisdom found a few common qualities, listed here: "Social reasoning, ability to give good advice, life knowledge, and life skills;"

"empathy, compassion, warmth, altruism, and a sense of fairness;" "introspection, insight, intuition, and self-knowledge and awareness;" "acknowledgement of and coping effectively with uncertainty;" and "regulation and self-control."[1] Recall that Xenophon's Socrates excelled in giving advice, and Plato's Socrates in asking questions. Self-control is covered by his treatment of temperance, and he showed his grasp on fairness and uncertainty throughout his trial. Across the differing portrayals, Socrates exhibited most of these traits.

Cicero was not the only Roman to depict Socrates. Plutarch is another, although he wrote in Greek. He makes an interesting witness to the historical reception of Socrates because he has access to sources that have become lost to us. For instance, he relates a story in "Morals" that the Megarians, a school descended from Socrates, believed that Socrates' divine sign was actually a sneeze![2] He also is a source of information from lost texts which portray Socrates in a bad light. Plutarch is best known for his parallel lives, biographies of Greek and Roman notables compared side by side for the moral edification of his readers. This is no different, in many ways, from how he treats Socrates. He tells of his steadfast dedication to justice in prison, his heroic death, and his brave actions in war.

Apuleius was a Roman philosopher and rhetorician who took great personal interest in Socrates. He wrote, among other things, *On Plato and his Doctrine* and *On the God of Socrates*. He is most famous for his *Metamorphoses,* or *Golden*

Ass. The main character of this work says that Apollo loved Socrates more than any other because he was the wisest.[3] Again, we see the reputation of Socrates as a wise man.

We get the general sense that Socrates was received quite well after his death. His dynamism as a philosopher was appreciated through his death and his discussions. He has even been compared with Jesus—and came out favorably. Both figures suffered an innocent death after a sham trial, gathered dedicated disciples, were particularly focused on ethics, and strangely, given their subsequent influence, never wrote anything down themselves. There are perhaps even more striking similarities we can list, but the important takeaway is that Socrates earned a near-religious reverence, as he was viewed as a type of Jesus.

But Socrates has his share of critics, as well. Probably the sharpest pushback came from Friedrich Nietzsche. In the *Twilight of the Idols* there are a number of critiques he lodged against Socrates, but let's focus on two in particular.[4] Because Socrates declared that he had been ill and asked for a cock at his death to sacrifice to the god of healing, this meant, according to Nietzsche, that life was a long and festering illness that needed to be cured. There was no real enthusiasm for the good or excellent things in life. Closely related to this was the Socratic focus on the soul, which amounted to a denigration and neglect of the body. The core of this criticism is that much of life requires the enjoyment and use of the body. It is not hard to see some merit in Nietzsche's criticism of Socrates on these points, especially the latter. Nietzsche attacked Socrates for holding up a version of truth and ethical behavior that was objective (rather than relative) and indicated that the body and physical realm are all we know and all we should care for, not the remote soul and Forms, which are valid critiques. Yet ad hominem gripes that he looked like a "typical criminal"—that is, attacks on Socrates' character—landed less cleverly and seemed over-the-top. Still, his criticisms breathed fresh life into the talk surrounding ancient philosophy, which in the 19th century "had become stagnant and dogmatic" and not very often contested.[5] Nietzsche's iconoclast nature, therefore, added some flavor to the discipline.

Action steps

What accounts for Socrates' legacy? It is hard to boil it down to one single thing. However, one thing stands out. Socrates' example of excellence, perseverance, and conviction affected many people, and this was only possible because Socrates had many relationships with these people. This will be our own legacy as well. After we have gone, the people we have known will keep our legacy going through their memories.

Good, happy, and accomplished people are remembered, with a fine legacy to speak of. But this does not account for the entirety of why Socrates was remembered. The additional element is that he recognized a life of happiness and virtue cannot be lived apart from family and friends. His circle of associates was not merely along for the ride. They were essential to his life; they were, in some sense, his life. You cannot live an examined life if others aren't examining you. You cannot live a happy life if the others around you are wretched. What are you doing to make the lives of those around you happy as well?

Making someone happy generally means anticipating their needs. What is one small thing you can do for a loved one today? This can be as simple as offering them your jacket if you notice them shivering and it's cold outside, or an umbrella when it's raining. You might also make them coffee in the morning or take the time to listen and actively respond when they talk about their day at work. Doing something nice for someone else will make you feel better about yourself, guaranteed.

Chapter summary

- The two areas in which Socrates has proved to be a great influence historically are the realm of his principled death and his philosophical dialogues.
- Socrates' reputation continued to grow after his death, resulting in a literary genre known as Socratic logoi comprised of Plato and Xenophon's writings about him, as well as those of several other authors whose works are now lost.

- In the Roman period, Socrates continued to exert influence as a man of exceeding wisdom.
- In the medieval Christian period, Socrates was viewed as a type of secular Christ.
- Nietzsche believed Socrates contemptible for his advocacy of objective truth and morality and his elevation of the soul at the expense of the body.

AFTERWORD

Who we are and who we want to be lie worlds apart for many of us. We look to others who are closer to the ideal, and by this admiration, we can pull ourselves closer to what we want to become. There are many lessons we can take away from Socrates, but what draws them together is this singular figure who was able to live out his principles in a way few ever have. Seemingly, there was no disconnect between Socrates' aspirations and who he actually was. This can be described as a consistency of character, a realization of the ideal, or a unity of his personality. Whatever we call it, we recognize in Socrates a person who lived a life we wish to have for ourselves.

Socrates was also seeking out knowledge. Knowledge is an absolute necessity for living well. We cannot live a good life without pursuing knowledge, because we do not know what we do not know—what is currently unknown might be holding us back in some way. Socratic curiosity, not only about other topics but other people, was the way in which he increased his knowledge.

This curiosity or wonder about the world also has another aspect: the idea that we must embrace our ignorance. Ignorance is not something to be ashamed of unless we let that ignorance linger on without being provoked by curiosity. Learning helps us in every facet of life, personal or professional.

The different Socratic schools each have a focused lesson for us. The Cynics tell us to focus on what is essential and not superficial; the Megarians remind us to be precise in our language; the Cyrenaics show us we can find pleasure in whatever circumstances we happen to be in; the Academic Skeptics encourage us to understand all sides of an issue; and the Stoics recognized that we need to focus on our own character instead of worrying about other things and people.

In Socrates' critique of writing, we see an important lesson about language and its relation to thought. The use of words, written or even spoken, does not necessarily require that we have a handle on the subject we are talking about. We have to be able to explain what we mean to different audiences, which not only requires we know the different kinds of people we are talking to, but also that we know the material so well that we can adapt it to the ability and experiences of different people.

Xenophon paints a very practical portrait of Socrates in which the philosopher emphasizes we should learn and learn broadly, but only so much as is necessary to make use of that knowledge in some way that is of benefit to us. Our pursuit of knowledge, in other words, should always be undertaken for the advancement of the life we are leading. This also means that we should be including our friends in the possession of our knowledge—sharing it with them and their sharing what they know with us.

From Plato, we gain great insight into how Socrates tackled problems. He would imagine the possible conclusions of a situation, and then derive a kind of solace, not from making any decision, but merely from laying out all the possible scenarios before his mind's eye. Another important lesson is that we need to have the humility to learn from other people and be willing to give them credit for teaching us. Socrates in Plato is always after self-knowledge, an understanding of the self in its most intimate ways. This includes understanding our weaknesses, strengths, motivations, turnoffs, and as much of our personality as we can.

The lesson of Aristophanes and Socrates concerns the importance of how we perceive ourselves through the lens of everyone else. Without a doubt, others will have different conceptions of who we are, not just among themselves, but in comparison to our self-assessment. This frees us to pursue our own projects because we can do nothing to change the opinions of others. Another important aspect of Socrates, as depicted in Aristophanes, is to remind us that we need to speak to people on their level, based on who they are, especially when attempting to persuade someone.

In the trial and death of Socrates, we see that public opinion was formed in part by Aristophanes. Some of the more significant charges against Socrates were the accusations that he corrupted the youth, introduced new gods, and took pay for teaching, all of which he denied. Socrates was a man of ultimate commitment. He was not only willing to live for his principles but also to die for them. His examined life, particularly the dramatic scenes of his trial and death, has been an inspirational subject of art for centuries.

The main teachings of Socrates revolve around virtue and knowledge. This is because virtue and knowledge relate directly to the pursuit of happiness. Happiness is what we should orient our entire energy toward, but this does mean trying to mindfully consume the good things in life, like pleasure, material goods, and sex, without going overboard. Rather than cultivate the virtues and knowledge that lead to happiness, we ought to focus on the soul. This means that whatever excellences exist in the soul, we should focus on them, cultivate them, and neglect the unimportant things around us.

Socrates' legacy lives on through his death, trial, and inspiring ethical philosophy. His life was so captivating that many writers, including those whose work is now lost, wrote works with Socrates as the main character. Socrates' moral and intellectual character was viewed as transcending any particular views he held, so that even among rival schools (such as Stoics and Cynics) or different places (such as Rome and Athens), he was held in the highest esteem. During the Christian period, he was often assimilated into a Christ-like figure.

Socrates has only grown more relevant over time. Not only has time vindicated him from the charges he faced at this trial, but he has made many people into better people through his example and philosophy. Far from corrupting the youth, he has enriched, improved, inspired, and challenged young and old alike. But none of this will affect us unless we look at his example, consider the many lessons he offers us, and apply them to our own lives. When we apply his words to our lives, we have to understand what he said and how he behaved. That's what this book has attempted to show you. It has also suggested ways Socrates can apply to you and how to apply his knowledge. But we cannot apply it for you. You must do so on your own, using your initiative for your own benefit. We have a long way to go, but Socratic humility and virtue will help us get there.

OVER 10,000 PEOPLE HAVE ALREADY SUBSCRIBED. DID YOU TAKE YOUR CHANCE YET?

In general, around 50% of the people who start reading do not finish a book. You are the exception, and we are happy you took the time.

To honor this, we invite you to join our exclusive Wisdom University newsletter. You cannot find this subscription link anywhere else on the web but in our books!

Upon signing up, you'll receive two of our most popular bestselling books, highly acclaimed by readers like yourself. We sell copies of these books daily, but you will receive them as a gift. Additionally, you'll gain access to two transformative short sheets and enjoy complimentary access to all our upcoming e-books, completely free of charge!

This offer and our newsletter are free; you can unsubscribe anytime.

Here's everything you get:

- ✓ How To Start Mind Mapping eBook — ($9.99 Value)
- ✓ The Art Of Game Theory eBook — ($9.99 Value)
- ✓ Break Your Thinking Patterns Sheet — ($4.99 Value)
- ✓ Flex Your Wisdom Muscle Sheet — ($4.99 Value)
- ✓ All our upcoming eBooks — ($199.80* Value)

Total Value: $229.76

Go to wisdom-university.net for the offer!

(Or simply scan the code with your camera)

*If you download 20 of our books for free, this would equal a value of 199.80$

THE PEOPLE BEHIND WISDOM UNIVERSITY

Christoph Maurer, Founder and CEO

Christoph has always been a voracious reader with a writing talent. A bit less common, he has also been fascinated by business since he was a child. Consequently, after earning his degree in business management, he chose publishing as a full-time career. With his good friend of over 15 years, Michael, he founded Wisdom University. The company aims to build the most reader-centric original publishing house possible and become a household brand trusted by its dear readers. Practicing what he preaches, Christoph spends a considerable amount of time reading every day, deeply influenced by the examples set by Charlie Munger and Warren Buffet.

Michael Meisner, Founder and CEO

When Michael ventured into publishing books on Amazon, he discovered that his favorite topics—the intricacies of the human mind and behavior—were often tackled in a way that's too complex and unengaging. Thus, he dedicated himself to making his ideal a reality: books that effortlessly inform, entertain, and resonate with readers' everyday experiences, enabling them to enact enduring positive changes in their lives. Together with like-minded people, this ideal became his passion and profession. Michael is primarily in charge of steering the operational side of Wisdom University, as he continues to improve and extend the business.

Claire M. Umali, Publishing Manager

Collaborative work lies at the heart of crafting books, and keeping everyone on the same page is an essential task. Claire oversees all the stages of this collaboration, from researching to outlining and from writing to editing. In her free time, she writes online reviews and likes to bother her cats.

Farley Bermeo, Publishing Manager

Farley has a knack for storytelling and writing personal narratives, both mundane and the extraordinary. Combining his background in writing and experience in program management, he ensures that ideas are transformed into pages. He believes that a good story is better told with a steaming cup of coffee.

Michael Moore, Writer

Michael Moore is a PhD researcher at the University of Chicago. His published books on philosophy include

Classical Philosophy in a Nutshell and Philosophy: 50 Essential Ideas.

Zoe Grabow, Co-Writer

Zoe is an "Everything Bagel" writer with a taste for fiction and nonfiction alike. Her BA in creative writing and philosophy often steers her toward Ancient Greece, having presented one paper on Aristotelian virtue ethics and then another comparing the tragic figures of Antigone and Socrates. A hopeless cinephile who gravitates towards Stephen King adaptations and anything Nolan, she also listens to Maria Callas while eating a big bowl of Fettucine under pesto and sometimes forgets to tie her sandals.

Andrew Speno, Content Editor

Andrew is a teacher, writer, and editor. He has published two historical nonfiction books for middle-grade readers, a biography of Eddie Rickenbacker and the story of the 1928 Bunion Derby ultra-marathon. He enjoys cooking, attending live theater, and playing the ancient game of go.

Sandra Agarrat, Language Editor

Sandra Wall Agarrat is an experienced freelance academic editor/proofreader, writer, and researcher. Sandra holds graduate degrees in Public Policy and International Relations. Her portfolio of projects includes books, dissertations, theses, scholarly articles, and grant proposals.

Mariah B. Girouard, Researcher

Mariah conducts careful research and creates thorough outlines that serve as the basis for Wisdom University's books. She is also a stand-up comedian, spoken word artist, tour guide, and travel writer. Mariah's passion for the arts and the world informs her work and what she produces for Wisdom University.

Ralph Escarda, Layout Designer

Ralph's love for books prevails in his artistic preoccupations. He is an avid reader of non-fictional books and an advocate of self-improvement through education. He dedicates his spare time to doing portraits and sports.

Alpia Villacorta, Layout Designer

Alpia makes sure that each book follows Wisdom University's formatting and design standards, helping it look outstanding, organized, and reader-friendly. She also helps curate suitable images for book covers. For Alpia, becoming an expert layout designer requires a lot of creativity and attention to detail. She believes that maintaining a positive and joyful attitude, along with reading self-help books, can aid in taking care of one's mental health.

Natalie Briggs, Copywriter

Natalie Briggs is a 20-year veteran of the Caribbean's mediascape, having worked as a journalist, editor, broadcaster, and producer in three countries. In 2020, she turned her hand to copywriting and has worked with Wisdom University for two of those three years. She is a graduate of the University of the West Indies and the University of Leicester. She holds a BA in History and Literature and an MA in PR and Communications.

Yusra Rafiq, Copywriter

Yusra Rafiq, a freelance content alchemist, crafts content across diverse niches. Her expertise, honed over three years, encompasses writing, SEO optimization, and a spectrum of digital content. Beyond work, Yusra finds joy in family, pets, and love for documentaries, true crime, and sci-fi.

Jemarie Gumban, Hiring Manager

Jemarie is in charge of thoroughly examining and evaluating the profiles and potential of the many aspiring writers and associates for Wisdom University. With an academic background in Applied Linguistics and a meaningful experience as an industrial worker, she approaches her work with a discerning eye and fresh outlook. Guided by her unique perspective, Jemarie derives fulfillment from turning a writer's desire to create motivational literature into tangible reality.

Evangeline Obiedo, Publishing Assistant

Evangeline diligently supports our books' journey, from the writing stage to connecting with our readers. Her commitment to detail permeates her work, encompassing tasks such as initiating profile evaluations and ensuring seamless delivery of our newsletters. Her love for learning extends into the real world—she loves traveling and experiencing new places and cultures.

REFERENCES

1. The Wisdom Of A Beginner's Mind

1. Plato. (1921). "Theaetetus," 149a-151a, 155d. *Plato in twelve volumes*, Vol. 12. (Harold N. Fowler, Trans.). Harvard University Press. The Perseus Catalog. https://www.perseus.tufts.edu/hopper/text?doc=Perseus%3Atext%3A1999.01.0172%3Atext%3DTheaet.%3Asection%3D155d
2. Chrysopoulos, P. (2023, November 25). *Socrates, the founder of Western philosophy*. Greek Reporter. https://greekreporter.com/2023/11/25/socrates-founder-of-western-philosophy/
3. Plato. (1968). "Laws," 10.902e. *Plato in twelve volumes*, Vols. 10 & 11. (R. G. Bury, Trans.). Harvard University Press. The Perseus Catalog. https://www.perseus.tufts.edu/hopper/text?doc=Perseus%3Atext%3A1999.01.0166%3Abook%3D10%3Asection%3D902e
4. Plato. (1966). "Phaedo," 61b, 97d-98e. *Plato in twelve volumes*, Vol. 1. (Harold North Fowler, Trans.) Harvard University Press. The Perseus Catalog. https://www.perseus.tufts.edu/hopper/text?doc=Perseus%3Atext%3A1999.01.0170%3Atext%3DPhaedo%3Asection%3D61b
5. Ancient Greece Facts.com. (n.d.). *Ancient Greece military and wars*. https://ancientgreecefacts.com/ancient-greece-military/#:~:text=Athenian%20soldiers%20were%20required%20to%20serve%20two%20years,called%20at%20any%20moment%20up%20to%20age%20sixty.
6. Plato. (1925). "Symposium," 220d-e. *Plato in twelve volumes*, Vol. 9. (Harold N. Fowler, Trans.). Harvard University Press. The Perseus Catalog. https://www.perseus.tufts.edu/hopper/text?doc=Perseus%3Atext%3A1999.01.0174%3Atext%3DSym.%3Asection%3D220d
7. Plato. (1955). "Laches," 181b. *Plato in twelve volumes*, Vol. 8. (W. R. M. Lamb, Trans.). Harvard University Press. The Perseus Catalog. https://www.perseus.tufts.edu/hopper/text?doc=Perseus%3Atext%3A1999.01.0176%3Atext%3DLach.%3Asection%3D181b
8. Fabiano, G., Marcellusi, A., & Favato, G. (2020). Channels and processes of knowledge transfer: How does knowledge move

between university and industry? *Science and Public Policy, 47*(2), 256-270, 264-5. https://doi.org/10.1093/scipol/scaa002
9. Argote, L., Guo, J., Park, S.-S., & Hahl, O. (2022). The mechanisms and components of knowledge transfer: The virtual special issue on knowledge transfer within organizations. *Organizational Science, 33*(3), 1232-1249, 1235-6. https://doi.org/10.1287/orsc.2022.1590
10. Xenophon. (1923). "Memorabilia," 2.3.7-9. *Xenophon in seven volumes*, Vol. 4. (E. C. Marchant, Trans.). Harvard University Press. The Perseus Catalog. http://www.perseus.tufts.edu/hopper/text?doc=Perseus%3Atext%3A1999.01.0208%3Abook%3D2%3Achapter%3D3%3Asection%3D7

2. Do You Know That You Don't Know?

1. Plato. (1966) "Apology," 20e-22b. *Plato in twelve volumes*, Vol. 1. (Harold North Fowler, Trans.). Harvard University Press. The Perseus Catalog. https://www.perseus.tufts.edu/hopper/text?doc=Perseus%3Atext%3A1999.01.0170%3Atext%3DApol.%3Asection%3D20e
2. Muller, A., Sirianni, L. A., & Addante, R. J. (2020). Neural correlates of the Dunning-Kruger effect. *European Journal of Neuroscience, 53*(2), p. 460-4, 460. https://doi.org/10.1111/ejn.14935
3. The Decision Lab. (n.d.). *Why do we think we understand the world more than we actually do?* https://thedecisionlab.com/biases/the-illusion-of-explanatory-depth
4. Cohn, A. (2021, February 15). Don't let self-doubt hold you back. *Harvard Business Review*. https://hbr.org/2021/02/dont-let-self-doubt-hold-you-back
5. Wichman, A., Brinol, P., Petty, R., Rucker, D., Tormala, Z., & Waery, G. (2010). Doubting one's doubt: A formula for confidence? *Journal of Experimental Social Psychology, 46*(2), p. 350-355, 351-4. https://doi.org/10.1016/j.jesp.2009.10.012
6. Yi, S. K. M., Steyvers, M., Lee, M. D., & Dry, M. J. (2012). The wisdom of the crowd in combinatorial problems. *Cognitive Science, 36*(3), p. 452-470, 452-469. https://doi.org/10.1111/j.1551-6709.2011.01223.x

3. Your 5 Keys To Unlocking Socrates

1. ESPN.com. (2013, May 22). *Coaching tree, legacy of Paul Brown.*

https://www.espn.com/nfl/story/_/page/coachingtree130522/greatest-nfl-coaches-paul-brown-coaching-tree
2. ESPN.com. (2013, June 10). *Coaching tree, legacy of Bill Walsh*. https://www.espn.com/nfl/story/_/page/coachingtreewalsh130610/greatest-nfl-coaches-bill-walsh-coaching-tree
3. Encyclopaedia Britannica. (1911). Antisthenes. In *Wikipedia*. Retrieved December 6, 2023, from https://en.wikisource.org/wiki/1911_Encyclop%C3%A6dia_Britannica/Antisthenes
4. Laertius, D. (1972). *Lives of eminent philosophers*, 2.8.66, 2.10.106, 6.1.9. (R. D. Hicks, Trans.). Harvard University Press. The Perseus Catalog. https://www.perseus.tufts.edu/hopper/text?doc=Perseus%3Atext%3A1999.01.0258%3Abook%3D6%3Achapter%3D1
5. History Skills. (n.d.). *Diogenes: The crazy, nudist Greek philosopher who insulted Alexander the Great*. https://www.historyskills.com/classroom/ancient-history/diogenes/
6. The Editors of Encyclopaedia Britannica. (n.d.). Megarian school. In *Encyclopaedia Britannica*. Retrieved December 6, 2023, from https://www.britannica.com/topic/Megarian-school
7. Boxell, L., Gentzkow, M., & Shapiro, J. M. (2021). Cross-country trends in affective polarization. *National Bureau of Economic Research*, 1-60, 1-18. https://doi.org/10.3386/w26669
8. The Editors of Encyclopaedia Britannica. (n.d.). Cyrenaic. In *Encyclopaedia Britannica*. Retrieved December 6, 2023, from https://www.britannica.com/topic/Cyrenaic
9. Stanford Encyclopedia of Philosophy. (2021). Arcesilaus. In *Stanford Encyclopedia of Philosophy*. Retrieved December 6, 2023, from https://plato.stanford.edu/entries/arcesilaus/
10. The Editors of Encyclopaedia Britannica. (n.d.). Epochē. In *Encyclopaedia Britannica*. Retrieved December 6, 2023, from https://www.britannica.com/topic/epoche
11. Saunders, J. L. (2023). Stoicism. In *Encyclopaedia Britannica*. https://www.britannica.com/topic/Stoicism
12. MacLellan, A. & Derakshan, N. (2021). The effects of Stoic training and adaptive working memory training on emotional vulnerability in high worriers. *Cognitive Therapy and Research 45*, 730-744, 734-740. https://doi.org/10.1007/s10608-020-10183-4
13. Birkbeck, University of London. (2020, December 4). *Birkbeck study on Stoicism and its impact on mental health*. https://www.bbk.ac.uk/news/birkbeck-study-on-stoicism-and-its-impact-on-mental-health-1

4. The Man Who Shunned Writing

1. Plato. (1925). "Phaedrus," 261c-262b, 270b-272b, 274c-276d. *Plato in twelve volumes*, Vol. 9. (Harold N. Fowler, Trans.). Harvard University Press. The Perseus Catalog. https://www.perseus.tufts.edu/hopper/text?doc=Perseus%3Atext%3A1999.01.0174%3Atext%3DPhaedrus%3Apage%3D262
2. Ransom, A., LaGrant, B., Spiteri, A., Kushnir, T., Anderson, A. K., & De Rosa, E. (2022). Face-to-face learning enhances the social transmission of information. *Plos One*, 1-17, 1. https://doi.org/10.1371/journal.pone.0264250
3. Stephens, G. J., Silbert, L. J., & Hasson, U. (2010). Speaker-listener neural coupling underlies successful communication. *PNAS 107*(32), 14425-14430, 14425-8. https://doi.org/10.1073/pnas.1008662107
4. Grujičić, R. (2023, October 30). *Prefrontal cortex*. KenHub. https://www.kenhub.com/en/library/anatomy/prefrontal-cortex

5. Enough Is Enough

1. Plato. (1921). "Theaetetus," 174a. *Plato in twelve volumes*, Vol. 12. (Harold N. Fowler, Trans.). Harvard University Press. The Perseus Catalog. https://www.perseus.tufts.edu/hopper/text?doc=Perseus%3Atext%3A1999.01.0172%3Atext%3DTheaet.%3Asection%3D174a
2. Aesop. (n.d.). The Astrologer. *The Æsop for children*. Library of Congress. https://www.read.gov/aesop/100.html
3. Xenophon. (1923). "Memorabilia," 4.5.10, 4.7.2-5. *Xenophon in seven volumes*, Vol. 4. (E. C. Marchant, Trans.). Harvard University Press. The Perseus Catalog. https://www.perseus.tufts.edu/hopper/text?doc=Perseus%3Atext%3A1999.01.0208%3Abook%3D4%3Achapter%3D5%3Asection%3D10
4. Strauss, L. (1970). *Xenophon's Socratic discourse: An interpretation of the Oeconomicus*, 1.13, 2.6, 3.1., 21.2-3 (Carnes Lord, Trans.). Cornell University Press. Internet Archive. https://archive.org/details/xenophonssocrati00stra_0/page/n5/mode/2up
5. Mueller-Bloch, C. & Kranz, J. (2015). A framework for rigorously identifying research gaps in qualitative literature reviews. *Proceedings of the 36th International Conference on Information Systems (ICIS)*, 1-19, 6. https://www.researchgate.net/publication/283271278_A_Framework_for_Rigorously_Identifying_Research_Gaps_in_Qualitative_Literature_Reviews.

6. Gourley, G. (2017, November 22). 10 tips for filling your knowledge gaps. *Medium.* https://medium.com/@geoffgourley/in-his-10-tips-for-filling-your-knowledge-gaps-34bad0b57573
7. Xenophon. (1979). "Symposium," 2.10, 3.3. *Xenophon in seven volumes*, Vol. 4. (O. J. Todd, Trans.). Harvard University Press. The Perseus Catalog. https://www.perseus.tufts.edu/hopper/text?doc=Perseus%3Atext%3A1999.01.0212%3Atext%3DSym.%3Achapter%3D2%3Asection%3D10
8. Bradley, D. (2022, February 24). Why Gladwell's 10,000-hour rule is wrong. *BBC.* https://www.bbc.com/future/article/20121114-gladwells-10000-hour-rule-myth
9. Kleim, J. A., Hogg, T. M., VandenBerg, P. M., Cooper, N. R., Bruneau, R., & Remple, M. (2004). Cortical synaptogenesis and motor map reorganization occur during late, but not early, phase of motor learning. *The Journal of Neuroscience: The Official Journal of the Society for Neuroscience, 24*(3), 628-33, 628. https://doi.org/10.1523/jneurosci.3440-03.2004
10. Oby, E. R., Golub, M. D., Hennig, J. A., Degenhart, A. D., Tyler-Kabara, E. C., Yu, B. M., Chase, S. M.,& Batista, A. P. (2019). New neural activity patterns emerge with long-term learning. *Proceedings of the National Academy of Sciences of the United States of America, 116*(30), 15210-15215, 15214. https://doi.org/10.1073/pnas.1820296116
11. Butts, D. A. & Goldman, M. S. (2006). Tuning Curves, Neuronal Variability, and Sensory Coding. *Plos Biology 4*(4), 0639-0646, 0639. https://doi.org/10.1371%2Fjournal.pbio.0040092

6. Plato's Socrates

1. Plato. (1966). "Phaedo," 96a-98b. *Plato in twelve volumes*, Vol. 1. (Harold North Fowler, Trans.). Harvard University Press. The Perseus Catalog. https://www.perseus.tufts.edu/hopper/text?doc=Perseus%3Atext%3A1999.01.0170%3Atext%3DPhaedo%3Asection%3D96a
2. Plato. (1966). "Apology," 40c-41c. *Plato in twelve volumes*, Vol. 1. (Harold North Fowler, Trans.). Harvard University Press. The Perseus Catalog. https://www.perseus.tufts.edu/hopper/text?doc=Perseus%3Atext%3A1999.01.0170%3Atext%3DApol.%3Asection%3D40c
3. Rezapour, M. (2022). The interactive factors contributing to fear of death. *Frontiers in Psychology 13*, 1-9, 6-7. https://doi.org/10.3389/fpsyg.2022.905594

4. Plato. (1925). "Symposium," 211c. *Plato in Twelve Volumes*, Vol. 9. (Harold N. Fowler, Trans.). Harvard University Press. The Perseus Catalog. https://www.perseus.tufts.edu/hopper/text?doc=Perseus%3Atext%3A1999.01.0174%3Atext%3DSym.%3Asection%3D211c
5. Plato. (1969). "Republic," 4.435b-441a. *Plato in twelve volumes*, Vols. 5 & 6. (Paul Shorey, Trans.). Harvard University Press. The Perseus Catalog. https://www.perseus.tufts.edu/hopper/text?doc=Perseus%3Atext%3A1999.01.0168%3Abook%3D4%3Asection%3D439b

7. Have You Ever Been The Butt Of The Joke?

1. Aristophanes. (1853). "Clouds," p. 123-4, 127, 156. *The comedies of Aristophanes*. (William James Hickie, Trans.). Bohn's Classical Library. https://en.wikisource.org/wiki/The_Comedies_of_Aristophanes_(Hickie_1853)/Clouds
2. Gruber, M. J., Gelman, B. D., & Ranganath, C. (2014). States of curiosity modulate hippocampus-dependent learning via the dopaminergic circuit. *Cell 84*(2), 486-96, 486. https://doi.org/10.1016/j.neuron.2014.08.060
3. Ocran, E. (2023, October 30). Nucleus accumbens. *Kenhub*. https://www.kenhub.com/en/library/anatomy/nucleus-accumbens-en
4. Ta, V. P. Boyd, R. L. Seraj, S., Keller, A., Griffith, C., Loggarakis, A., & Medema, L. (2022). An inclusive, real-world investigation of persuasion in language and verbal behavior. *Journal of Computational Social Science, 5*(1), p. 883-903, 892-6. https://doi.org/10.1007/s42001-021-00153-5
5. Klucharev, V. Smidts, A., & Fernández, G. (2008). Brain mechanisms of persuasion: How 'expert power' modulates memory and attitudes. *Social Cognitive and Affective Neuroscience 3*(4), 353-366, 353-361. https://doi.org/10.1093/scan/nsn022
6. Bandoim, L. (2023, September 13). *The anatomy of the prefrontal cortex*. Verywell Health. https://www.verywellhealth.com/prefrontal-cortex-5220699
7. Cleveland Clinic. (n.d.). Temporal lobe. Retrieved December 8, 2023, from https://my.clevelandclinic.org/health/body/16799-temporal-lobe

8. The Trial Of Socrates

1. Plato. (1966). "Apology," 17d, 19b-c, 21d, 23c-24d, 25c-d, 26a-28d, 29d, 30c-31d, 35c-37e, 40a-42a. *Plato in twelve volumes*, Vol. 1. (Harold North Fowler, Trans.). Harvard University Press. The Perseus Catalog. https://www.perseus.tufts.edu/hopper/text?doc=Perseus%3Atext%3A1999.01.0170%3Atext%3DApol.%3Asection%3D23c
2. Plato. (1966). "Euthyphro," 2b, 5a-b. *Plato in twelve volumes*, Vol. 1. (Harold North Fowler, Trans.). Harvard University Press. The Perseus Catalog. https://www.perseus.tufts.edu/hopper/text?doc=Perseus%3Atext%3A1999.01.0170%3Atext%3DEuthyph.%3Asection%3D2b
3. UMKC School of Law. (n.d.). *The three accusers of Socrates.* Trial of Socrates. http://law2.umkc.edu/faculty/projects/ftrials/socrates/accusers.html
4. Plato. (1967). "Meno," 94a-95a. *Plato in twelve volumes*, Vol. 3. (W. R. M. Lamb, Trans.). Harvard University Press. The Perseus Catalog. https://www.perseus.tufts.edu/hopper/text?doc=Perseus%3Atext%3A1999.01.0178%3Atext%3DMeno%3Asection%3D94a
5. Plato. (1966). "Crito," 43a-50c. *Plato in twelve volumes*, Vol. 1. (Harold North Fowler, Trans.). Harvard University Press. The Perseus Catalog. https://www.perseus.tufts.edu/hopper/text?doc=Perseus%3Atext%3A1999.01.0170%3Atext%3DCrito%3Asection%3D43a
6. Plato. (1966). "Phaedo," 70d-77b, 78a-80b, 100b-107a, 117e-118a. *Plato in twelve volumes*, Vol. 1. (Harold North Fowler, Trans.). Harvard University Press. The Perseus Catalog. https://www.perseus.tufts.edu/hopper/text?doc=Perseus%3Atext%3A1999.01.0170%3Atext%3DPhaedo%3Asection%3D70d
7. Vicente, R., Rizzuto, M., Sarica, C., Yamamoto, K., Sadr, M., Khajuria, T., Fatehi, M., Moien-Afshari, F., Haw, C. S., Llinas, R. R., Lozano, A. M., Neimat, J. S., & Zemmar, A. (2022). Enhanced interplay of neuronal coherence and coupling in the dying human brain. *Frontiers in Aging Neuroscience, 14*, 1-11, 1, 8-9. https://doi.org/10.3389/fnagi.2022.813531
8. Larson, J. (2020, June 22). *What to know about gamma brain waves.* Healthline. https://www.healthline.com/health/gamma-brain-waves
9. Larson, J. (2019, October 9). *What are alpha brain waves and why are they important?* Healthline. https://www.healthline.com/health/alpha-brain-waves

10. Xenophon. (1979). "Apology," 6. *Xenophon in seven volumes*, Vol. 4. (O. J. Todd, Trans.). Harvard University Press. The Perseus Catalog. https://www.perseus.tufts.edu/hopper/text?doc=Perseus%3Atext%3A1999.01.0212%3Atext%3DApol.%3Asection%3D6
11. Truman, J. (n.d.). *Why did Aristotle leave Athens? A historical perspective*. DeepThinkers: The Encyclopedia of Philosophy. https://www.deepthinkers.net/why-did-aristotle-leave-athens-a-historical-perspective/
12. The Editors of Encyclopaedia Britannica. (2023, November 18). Academy. In *Encyclopaedia Britannica*. Retrieved December 8, 2023, from https://www.britannica.com/topic/Academy-ancient-academy-Athens-Greece
13. Hegel, G. W. F. (1892). *Hegel's lectures on the history of philosophy in three volumes*, Vol. 1, p. 411-423, 433-434. (E. S. Haldane, Trans.). Kegan Paul, Trench, Trübner & Co. Ltd. The Project Gutenberg. https://www.gutenberg.org/cache/epub/51635/pg51635-images.html#c397
14. Nietzsche, F. (1910). *The Birth of Tragedy or Hellenism and Pessimism*, p. 114, 116-7. (WM. A. Haussmann, Trans.). George Allen & Unwin Ltd. The Project Gutenberg. https://www.gutenberg.org/files/51356/51356-h/51356-h.htm
15. Periyakoil, V. S., Neri, E., & Kraemer, H. (2018). Common items on a bucket list. *Journal of Palliative Medicine, 21*(5). https://doi.org/10.1089/jpm.2017.0512

9. Socrates' Blueprint To Real Happiness

1. Plato. (1969). "Republic," 1.354a. *Plato in twelve volumes*, Vols. 5 & 6. (Paul Shorey, Trans.). Harvard University Press. The Perseus Catalog. https://www.perseus.tufts.edu/hopper/text?doc=Perseus%3Atext%3A1999.01.0168%3Abook%3D1%3Asection%3D354a
2. Kaufman, S. B. & Jauk, E. (2020). Healthy selfishness and pathological altruism: Measuring two paradoxical forms of selfishness. *Frontiers in Psychology 11*, 1-16, 13. https://doi.org/10.3389/fpsyg.2020.01006
3. Waldinger, R. J. & Schulz, M. S. (2010). What's love got to do with it?: Social functioning, perceived health, and daily happiness in married octogenarians. *Psychology and Aging 25*(2), 422-431. https://doi.org/10.1037/a0019087
4. Plato. (1955). "Laches," 190c. *Plato in twelve volumes*, Vol. 8. (W. R. M. Lamb, Trans.). Harvard University Press. The Perseus Catalog.

https://www.perseus.tufts.edu/hopper/text?doc=Perseus:text:1999.01.0176:text=Lach.:section=190c
5. Plato. (1969). "Republic," 7.536a-b. *Plato in twelve volumes*, Vols. 5 & 6. (Paul Shorey, Trans.). Harvard University Press. The Perseus Catalog. https://www.perseus.tufts.edu/hopper/text?doc=Perseus%3Atext%3A1999.01.0168%3Abook%3D7%3Asection%3D536a
6. Plato. (1966). "Apology," 30a. *Plato in twelve volumes*, Vol. 1. (Harold North Fowler, Trans.). Harvard University Press. The Perseus Catalog. https://www.perseus.tufts.edu/hopper/text?doc=Perseus%3Atext%3A1999.01.0170%3Atext%3DApol.%3Asection%3D30a
7. Plato. (1967). "Gorgias," 469b-c. *Plato in twelve volumes*, Vol. 3. (W. R. M. Lamb, Trans.). Harvard University Press. The Perseus Catalog. https://www.perseus.tufts.edu/hopper/text?doc=Perseus%3Atext%3A1999.01.0178%3Atext%3DGorg.%3Asection%3D469b
8. Bethell, C. D., Gombojav, N., & Whitaker, R. C. (2019). Family resilience and connection promote flourishing among US children, even amid adversity. *Health Affairs 38*(5), 729-737, 729-731. https://doi.org/10.1377/hlthaff.2018.05425

10. Who's The Wisest Of Them All?

1. Bangen, K. J., Meeks, T. W., Jeste, D. V. (2013). Defining and assessing wisdom: A review of the literature. *The American Journal of Geriatric Psychiatry: Official Journal of the American Association for Geriatric Psychiatry, 21*(12), 1254-1266. https://doi.org/10.1016/j.jagp.2012.11.020
2. Plutarch. (1874). *Plutarch's Morals*, 12. Little, Brown, and Company. The Perseus Catalog. https://www.perseus.tufts.edu/hopper/text?doc=Perseus%3Atext%3A2008.01.0306%3Asection%3D11
3. Apuleius, L. (1639). *Metamorphoses*, 10.46. (William Adlington, Trans.). The Project Gutenberg. https://www.gutenberg.org/files/1666/1666-h/1666-h.htm#link2H_4_0056
4. Nietzsche, F. W. (1911). *Twilight of the Idols*, p. 9-11. (Anthony M. Ludovici, Trans.). T. N. Foulis. The Project Gutenberg. https://www.gutenberg.org/files/52263/52263-h/52263-h.htm
5. Kjeldsen, K. J. L. (2020, August 31). Nietzsche vs. Socrates. *Noontide Magazine*. https://medium.com/noontide/nietzsche-versus-socrates-d67ebd727d5d

DISCLAIMER

The information contained in this book and its components, is meant to serve as a comprehensive collection of strategies that the author of this book has done research about. Summaries, strategies, tips and tricks are only recommendations by the author, and reading this book will not guarantee that one's results will exactly mirror the author's results.

The author of this book has made all reasonable efforts to provide current and accurate information for the readers of this book. The author and their associates will not be held liable for any unintentional errors or omissions that may be found, and for damages arising from the use or misuse of the information presented in this book.

Readers should exercise their own judgment and discretion in interpreting and applying the information to their specific circumstances. This book is not intended to replace professional advice (especially medical advice, diagnosis, or treatment). Readers are encouraged to seek appropriate professional guidance for their individual needs.

The material in the book may include information by third parties. Third party materials comprise of opinions expressed by their owners. As such, the author of this book does not assume responsibility or liability for any third party material or opinions.

The publication of third party material does not constitute the author's guarantee of any information, products, services, or opinions contained within third party material. Use of third party material does not guarantee that your results will mirror our results. Publication of such third party material is simply a recommendation and expression of the author's own opinion of that material.

Whether because of the progression of the Internet, or the unforeseen changes in company policy and editorial submission guidelines, what is stated as fact at the time of this writing may become outdated or inapplicable later.

Wisdom University is committed to respecting copyright laws and intellectual property rights. We have taken reasonable measures to ensure that all quotes, diagrams, figures, images, tables, and other information used in this publication are either created by us, obtained with permission, or fall under fair use guidelines. However, if any copyright infringement has inadvertently occurred, please notify us promptly at wisdom-university@mail.net, providing sufficient details to identify the specific material in question. We will take immediate action to rectify the situation, which may include obtaining necessary permissions, making corrections, or removing the material in subsequent editions or reprints.

This book is copyright ©2023 by Wisdom University with all rights reserved. It is illegal to redistribute, copy, or create derivative works from this book whole or in parts. No parts of this report may be reproduced or retransmitted in any forms whatsoever without the written expressed and signed permission from the publisher.